Continuity and Change in the Rhetoric of the Moral Majority

PRAEGER SERIES IN POLITICAL
COMMUNICATION
Robert E. Denton, Jr., *General Editor*

Continuity and Change in the Rhetoric of the Moral Majority

David Snowball

Praeger Series in Political Communication

PRAEGER

New York
Westport, Connecticut
London

Library of Congress Cataloging-in-Publication Data

Snowball, David.
   Continuity and change in the rhetoric of the Moral Majority /
David Snowball.
         p.   cm. — (Praeger series in political communication)
   Includes bibliographical references and index.
   ISBN 0-275-93689-9
   1. Moral Majority, Inc. 2. Fundamentalism. 3. Christianity and
politics. 4. Evangelicalism—United States—History—20th century.
5. Conservatism—United States—History—20th century. 6. Falwell,
Jerry. 7. United States—Politics and government—1977-1981.
8. United States—Politics and government—1981-1989. 9. United
States—Church history—20th century.   I. Title. II. Series.
BT82.2.S68 1991
322.4'4'0973—dc20   90-45196

British Library Cataloguing in Publication Data is available.

Library of Congress Catalog Card Number: 90-45196
ISBN: 0-275-93689-9

First published in 1991

Praeger Publishers, One Madison Avenue, New York, NY 10010
An imprint of Greenwood Publishing Group, Inc.

Printed in the United States of America

The paper used in this book complies with the
Permanent Paper Standard issued by the National
Information Standards Organization (Z39.48-1984).

10 9 8 7 6 5 4 3 2 1

This work is dedicated to the three people who made it possible, necessary, and inevitable:

William Joseph Snowball, who read to me and taught me to love learning and to find joy in the printed word.

Dorothy Louise Snowball, who loved and nurtured the strange little kid who would rather read on the front porch swing than do normal kid-things.

Linda Roy Snowball, who prodded, bullied, teased, edited and cajoled a dissertation, a book, and a career out of me when I thought it would be a lot easier just to sleep in.

Contents

Series Foreword

Those of us from the discipline of communication studies have long believed that communication is prior to all other fields of inquiry. In several other forums I have argued that the essence of politics is "talk" or human interaction.[1] Such interaction may be formal or informal, verbal or nonverbal, public or private, but always persuasive, forcing us consciously or subconsciously to interpret, to evaluate, and to act. Communication is the vehicle for human action.

From this perspective, it is not surprising that Aristotle recognized the natural kinship of politics and communication in his writings of *Politics* and *Rhetoric*. In the former, he establishes that humans are "political beings [who] alone of the animals [are] furnished with the faculty of language."[2] In the latter, he begins his systematic analysis of discourse by proclaiming that "rhetorical study, in its strict sense, is concerned with the modes of persuasion."[3] Thus, it was recognized over 2,000 years ago that politics and communication go hand in hand because they are essential parts of human nature.

Back in 1981, Dan Nimmo and Keith Sanders proclaimed that political communication was an emerging field.[4] Although its origin, as noted, dates back centuries, a "self-consciously cross-disciplinary" focus began in the late 1950s. Thousands of books and articles later, colleges and universities offer a variety of graduate and undergraduate coursework in the area in such diverse departments as communication, mass communication, journalism, political science, and sociology.[5] In Nimmo and Sanders's early assessment, the "key areas of inquiry" included rhetorical analysis, propaganda analysis, attitude change studies, voting studies, government and the news media, functional and systems analyses, technological changes, media technologies, campaign techniques, and research techniques.[6] In a survey of the state of the field in 1983 by the same authors and Lynda Kaid, they found additional, more specific areas of concerns, such as the presidency, political polls, public opinion, debates, and advertising, to name a few.[7] Since the first study, they also noted a shift away from the rather strict behavioral approach.

Today, Dan Nimmo and David Swanson assert that "political communication has developed some identity as a more or less distinct domain of scholarly work."[8] The scope and concerns of the area have further expanded to include critical theories and cultural studies. While there is no precise definition, method, or disciplinary home of the area of inquiry, its primary domain is the role, processes, and effects of communication within the context of politics broadly defined.

In 1985, the editors of *Political Communication Yearbook: 1984* noted that "more things are happening in the study, teaching, and practice of political communication than can be captured within the space limitations of the relatively few publications available."[9] In addition, they argued that the backgrounds of "those involved in the field [are] so varied and plurist in outlook and approach, . . . it [is] a mistake to adhere slavishly to any set format in shaping the content."[10] More recently, Swanson and Nimmo called for "ways of overcoming the unhappy consequences of fragmentation within a framework that respects, encourages, and benefits from diverse scholarly commitments, agendas, and approaches."[11]

In agreement with these assessments of the area and with gentle encouragement, Praeger established the series entitled "Praeger Studies in Political Communication." The series is open to all qualitative and quantitative methodologies as well as contemporary and historical studies. The key to characterizing the studies in the series is the focus on communication variables or activities within a political context or dimension.

This fascinating study examines the rise and fall of the Moral

Majority. The book describes and interprets the ideas and strategies of the organization, and its contributions to the conservative movement. This powerful conservative political organization struck fear in the hearts of numerous members of Congress and the Senate. The organization single-handedly changed the political landscape in America, not so much in deeds as in words. It shaped the national debate of political issues and values preparing the way for the "Reagan Revolution."

This study makes several important contributions to the field of political communication. First, this effort is one of the few scholarly investigations of the Moral Majority. With an even and balanced treatment, the author provides an insightful analysis of the genesis, role, function, and "failure" of the organization. As a landmark study, it is destined to be an indispensible resource for serious scholars of the Moral Majority. Second, this book is a valuable addition to the study of contemporary social movements. In fact, it challenges some of the common assumptions about the rise and fall of movements. Especially insightful is understanding how a single individual and organization can initiate and sustain support within a larger social movement. Snowball provides a framework for comparing the life cycles of contemporary movements to much earlier ones. Finally, this book contributes to our overall understanding of politics of the 1980s. For some political observers, the 1980s were a watershed decade in American politics culminating in a new Republican majority and conservative dominated politics. Without doubt, the Moral Majority played an important role in the perceived transformation of the American electorate.

I am, without shame or modesty, a fan of the series. The joy of serving as its editor is in participating in the dialogue of the field of political communication and in reading the contributors' works. I invite you to join me.

Robert E. Denton, Jr.

NOTES

1. See Robert E. Denton, Jr., *The Symbolic Dimensions of the American Presidency* (Prospect Heights, IL: Waveland Press, 1982); Robert E. Denton, Jr. and Gary Woodward, *Political Communication in America*

(New York: Praeger, 1985, 2d ed., 1990); Robert E. Denton, Jr. and Dan Hahn, *Presidential Communication* (New York: Praeger, 1986); and Robert E. Denton, Jr., *The Primetime Presidency of Ronald Reagan* (New York: Praeger, 1988).

2. Aristotle, *The Politics of Aristotle*, trans. Ernest Barker (New York: Oxford University Press, 1970), p. 5.

3. Aristotle, *Rhetoric*, trans. Rhys Roberts (New York: The Modern Library, 1954), p. 22.

4. Dan Nimmo and Keith Sanders, "Introduction: The Emergence of Political Communication as a Field," in *Handbook of Political Communication*, Dan Nimmo and Keith Sanders, eds. (Beverly Hills, CA: Sage, 1981), pp. 11-36.

5. Ibid., p. 15.

6. Ibid., pp. 17-27.

7. Keith Sanders, Lynda Kaid, and Dan Nimmo, eds. *Political Communication Yearbook: 1984* (Carbondale, IL: Southern Illinois University, 1985), pp. 283-308.

8. Dan Nimmo and David Swanson, "The Field of Political Communication: Beyond the Voter Persuasion Paradigm" in *New Directions in Political Communication*, David Swanson and Dan Nimmo, eds. (Beverly Hills, CA: Sage, 1990), p. 8.

9. Sanders, Kaid, and Nimmo, *Political Communication*, p. xiv.

10. Ibid., p. xiv.

11. Nimmo and Swanson, *New Directions*, p. 11.

Preface

This book examines the life, rhetoric, and death of the Moral Majority, a conservative political organization with strong religious ties. The organization dominated the popular mind in the early 1980s and dissolved a decade later. While many people hailed its death, few paused to understand its life.

This work arises from my interest in examining how political systems respond to stress. The Moral Majority arose out of a period of national doubt and economic disarray, and it represented the concerns of many disenfranchised Americans. Our nation has, traditionally, not responded rationally to such movements. People tend either to demonize or deify the movement, responding with their hearts rather than their heads. In exploring the rhetoric of the Moral Majority and the persuasive strategies it followed, I hope to better explain the nature, constraints, and limits of political rationality in contemporary America.

In acknowledging contributions to a work, it is customary to recognize a body of people and then to reassure the reader that whatever errors remain in the book are the sole fault of the author. In my case, however, there are three people whose criticisms and insights have become so integral to my argument that they cannot escape either my guilt or my innocence in this work. Whether you decide that this work is lunatic or luminescent, it was materially abetted by Ronald F. Reid, Nicholas F.S. Burnett, and Linda Roy-Snowball. If you want to complain, one of them will be delighted to speak with you. Really.

Beyond these, there was a great number of people who lent guidance and assistance: Jane Blankenship and Milton Cantor, fine scholars and good people; Russell File, archivist at Liberty University; Ted Derrick, administrative editor of the *Moral Moral Report*; the librarians at the University of Massachusetts and Augustana College; and my colleagues from graduate school, who lent support when it was needed and criticism the rest of the time.

Continuity and Change in the Rhetoric of the Moral Majority

Chapter One

Overview of a Controversy

The great strength of the New Christian Right during the first half of the 1980s has been its rhetoric.
Jeffrey K. Hadden, sociologist, 13 June 1986[1]

We have had our excesses. . . we have been careless with our rhetoric.
Jerry Falwell, 13 March 1985[2]

The Moral Majority was an odd lot. Except for having an enormously presumptuous name, there was no reason that it should have garnered more attention than any of a dozen other "New Christian Right" groups, but it did. It was damned a hundred times for things its members said and for things they did not say. They were attacked for the way they said what they said and, at times, for things that were said by groups having nothing to do with the Moral Majority. They were even attacked for things that they never said, but that people suspected they might secretly have been thinking. However, for every attack they suffered, they raised 1,000 supporters and $1 million.

In retrospect, this might have been much ado about nothing. The Moral Majority certainly raised a lot of things: issues, blood pressure, money, political consciousness. Also, it is inseparably identified with the sweeping political changes of the late 1970s and early 1980s. Its name became a generic term for any narrowly intolerant group. The Reverend Falwell was identified as one of the most powerful figures in America in the early 1980s, but its candidates all lost. Its legislative initiatives uniformly failed. Its leader ended up joking and dining with Ted Kennedy, the man who could have been elected as the Anti-Christ at any Moral Majority gathering. What happened?

The Moral Majority was a conservative political action organization with conventional goals. It wanted to strengthen the Judeo-Christian foundations of the political system by generating popular pressure on elected officials and corporate executives. The Moral Majority was founded in June of 1979 by the Reverend Jerry Falwell, pastor of the Thomas Road Baptist Church in Lynchburg, Virginia. Falwell also hosted the "Old-Time Gospel Hour," a nationally televised Sunday worship service. Falwell located the decision to found his group in a backlash against liberal politics:

Our response to these seventeen years of liberal insensitivity to pro-moral concerns was not only to cry "enough," but also to stop crying and organize to do something about it. Thus, Moral Majority, Inc., was born and grew faster than any of us could have predicted.[3]

While the group's growth was rapid, its decline was painful and prolonged. Within seven years after its founding, Falwell seemed to abolish the Moral Majority by subsuming it within a new group, the Liberty Federation. While denying that the name change represented any sort of retreat, Falwell granted that the name "Moral Majority" had been so "bloodied and beaten" that the organization could no longer operate effectively.[4] Over the next three years, the group seesawed in and out of existence, undergoing revivals and dismissals as Falwell struggled to regain the political pre-eminence he had enjoyed years before.

The Moral Majority spent its years at the center of remarkably intense controversy. While it was neither the most affluent nor the most radical of the groups in the New Right, it nonetheless provoked the most ferocious responses, ranging from the millennial visions of its most ardent adherents to nearly hysterical denunciations from both the Left and the Right. The Moral Majority served both as an avatar of the Christian Right and a lightning rod for its critics, yet the organization itself has virtually escaped objective analysis.

The two theses defended here are simple: first, the rhetoric of the Moral Majority mattered. The organization existed only for its rhetoric. Second, it eventually failed because it could not find the words that would be acceptable to both its most devoted followers and to a broader spectrum of the American public. In this first chapter, we will look at four broad topics: (1) the popular and scholarly responses to the Moral Majority; (2) the background and nature of source materials available for constructing a rhetorical analysis of the Moral Majority; (3) the way that the Moral Majority described itself and its mission; and (4) the approach we will take in examining continuity and change in the rhetoric of the Moral Majority. This will provide the foundation for constructing and understanding the arguments that are to follow.

LITERATURE ON THE MORAL MAJORITY

The responses to the Moral Majority were premised on what the organization was suspected to be and on what it might become. It was suspected of being a secretive, anti-American, theocratic cabal. A better sense of history might have led Falwell to the ironic recognition that these were the very charges leveled by his ideological forebears against both Catholics and Jews.

Beginning in 1980, public discussion concerning the Moral Majority took on a hysterical tone. In a speech denouncing the Moral Majority, Patricia Harris, then Secretary of Health and Human Services, said that, "I am beginning to fear that we could have an Ayatollah Khomeini in this country."[5] Nicholas von Hoffman, a liberal columnist, decried Falwell's forces as "these Christian Stalinists" and went on to complain that: "The born-again ayatollahs preaching fundamentalist pugnacity on our television are as impervious to the give-and-take rationality of sane politicians as the old boy with the X-ray eyes in Tehran."[6]

That same year, Representative Parren Mitchell of Maryland chose to compare Falwell's tactics with those of the French revolutionist Robespierre, and alleged that

there are a few extremists who presume to influence the Congress— namely, the Rev. Jerry Falwell and the Moral Majority and John Dolan of the National Conservative Political Action Committee (NCPAC). These men are intent upon purging the element of pluralism and free expression from our democratic society.[7]

John Jenkins, writing in *The Humanist*, was scarcely more sanguine when he opined that "Jerry Falwell is emerging as the potential dictator of the New Christian Nation."[8] Even as the Moral Majority reeled in economic chaos in 1985, one author still felt safe in reiterating Jenkin's judgment, predicting that Falwell would be one of "tomorrow's tyrants."[9]

The most widely disseminated assault on Falwell came from A. Bartlett Giamatti, Yale University's president. In addressing the Class of 1985, Giamatti first discussed the values of a liberal education to the individual and society:

Its goal is to train the whole person to be at once intellectually discerning and humanly flexible, tough-minded and open-hearted; to be responsible to the new and responsible for the values that make us civilized.[10]

A little later, Giamatti turned to the role that the Moral Majority played in denying those values:

A self-proclaimed "Moral Majority" and its satellite or client groups, cunning in the use of a native blend of old intimidation and new technology, threaten the values I have named. Angry at change, rigid in the application of chauvinistic slogans, absolutistic in morality, they threaten through political pressure or public denunciation whoever dares to disagree with their authoritarian positions . . . there is no debate, no discussion, no dissent. They *know*.

Giamatti's complaint was typical of much of the response to Falwell's group: it imputed an overriding meanness of spirit and a desire to dominate through media manipulation. More importantly, it identified the Moral Majority's central heresy: rigid rejection of the views and values of those with whom it disagreed. Giamatti's address prompted predictable attacks from defenders of the New Right (including William F. Buckley, Jr., who suggested that Giamatti could teach Falwell "a thing or two about how one fulminates in the big league"[11]) and rejoinders from sympathetic liberal columnists (including Anthony Lewis, who suggested that Buckley's inaccurate invocation of a Biblical passage in defense of Falwell showed a willingness to distort the Word in the service of partisanship[12]).

Not all of the anti-Falwell reaction was generated by the liberals. The curmudgeonly James J. Kilpatrick described Falwell as a "saw-dust apostle" and suggested that "by and large, the Reverend Dr. Falwell, his brethren and sistren, give me the willies."[13] Kilpatrick balanced his distaste for Falwell by advancing his equal distaste for most of Falwell's opponents and concluded that the Reverend Doctor had an unassailable right to do just as he had been doing. Other conservative critics were less sure. Senator Barry Goldwater expressed his abhorrence:

I can say with conviction that the religious issues of these groups have little or nothing to do with conservative or liberal politics. The uncompromising position of these groups is a divisive element that could tear apart the very spirit of our representative system, if they gain sufficient strength.[14]

The Senator concluded that

the religious factions will go on imposing their will on others unless the decent people connected with them recognize that religion has no place in public policy. They must learn to make their views known without trying to make their views the *only* alternative.[15]

The New Right's response to Senator Goldwater was both harsh and broad-ranging: they varied from pitying suggestions about the Senator's dotage and the effects of constant pain from a bad hip to accusations that Goldwater was betraying the conservative cause and was hypocritically repudiating the very issues and tactics that he himself had pioneered in 1963 and 1964.[16] Both the Kilpatrick and Goldwater responses illustrated a common theme in conservative condemnations of Falwell: a combination of disdain for Falwell, the man, and an attack on his interjection of religion into politics.

A second type of public reaction to Falwell's emergence was a counterorganizing move among liberal forces. Organizations such as the Progressive Political Action Committee, Americans for Common Sense (organized by former senator George McGovern), People for the American Way (founded by television producer Norman Lear), and such lesser-known groups as Moral Alternatives, the Thinking Majority, the Real Majority, and the Interchange Resource Center were all created in response to the New Right in general and, as some of the names suggest, to the Moral Majority in particular. These groups did not become significant political forces, but they did herald the entry of leftist-moderate groups into territory previously held exclusively by the New Right.[17]

A third type of public reaction, which began around 1982, was a spate of popular books. We can place them into three rough classes: epideictic, political-analytic, and social-analytic. The first class involved books that were written for the express purpose of damning or celebrating the Moral Majority's efforts. Example of the former included books such as Perry Young's *God's Bullies*, Daniel Maguire's *The New Subversives: Anti-Americanism of the Religious Right*, Phillip Finch's *God, Guts and Guns*, and Flo Conway's *Holy Terror: The Fundamentalist War on America's Freedoms in Religion, Politics and Our Private Lives*.[18] One passage from Maguire's work can serve to illustrate the genre. At the end of the last substantive chapter of the book, Maguire concludes:

The New Right's "family" interests actually take us far from the hearth. It reveals a political plan to dominate women and children. It allows government control of the womb. It excommunicates some ten million homosexual citizens from their civil rights. It perverts the notion of majority rule in the democratic process. It points us toward the model of a fascist family in a fascist state. And all of this in the blessed name of "family."[19]

We can get an idea of how hostile the responses were by considering the fact that one book reviewer actually praised Maguire for avoiding the errors of paranoia and scapegoating in this book.[20]

At the opposite end of the continuum was a far smaller contingent of pro-Falwell works, such as William Willoughby's *Does*

America Need the Moral Majority?, Patricia Pingry's *Jerry Falwell: Man of Vision*, and Dinesh D'Souza's *Falwell: Before the Millennium*.[21] A representative excerpt came from Willoughby:

> The 1980 election isn't a one-time thing. Moral Majority will not merely fade away. The second shot to be heard around the world has been fired. The Second American Revolution has begun. A second Boston Tea Party has been held . . . [the Moral Majority's] voice is ringing throughout the land. The moral revolution is on.[22]

D'Souza issued the concurring judgment that Falwell was a leader "standing at the crossroads of history."[23]

The political-analytic works devoted themselves to determining whether groups such as the Moral Majority had or might come to have any serious political power. The general conclusion advanced by these authors was that the New Christian Right had very little direct political impact, and that stories to the contrary represented the bitter reactions of defeated politicians or the hysteria of a largely hostile press. Many of the articles did, however, admit that Falwell might have represented for a large number of unhappy, alienated people and that he should be attended to as being symptomatic of a serious problem.[24]

Finally, the social-analytic works tried to understand what brought the Moral Majority about and what its intellectual roots were. These works sometimes contained surprising insights that had escaped the attention of "serious" scholars; they noted, for example, that Falwell had at least three distinct audiences, that he varied his appeal for each audience, that his political concerns were undergirded by the particular psychology of fundamentalist Christians, and that his positions had evolved with time.[25] These articles were often well-written and serious, but they appeared only infrequently. As a result, they could not be relied upon to keep up with the changes in the Moral Majority.

While the popular writers were busy praising, condemning, and occasionally analyzing the Moral Majority, scholarly reaction was noticeable mainly by its absence. While approximately 300 indexed magazine articles appeared in the popular press between 1979 and 1985, only five articles appeared in the scholarly journals. Only two of these dealt with the Moral

Majority's rhetoric. There were also five dissertations on the Moral Majority's rhetoric and a handful of convention papers.[26]

In short, response to the Moral Majority was both profuse and limited. Popular writers were prolific, but scholars did little. Worse yet, much of the scholarly writing was of uneven quality, often taking on the hysterical tone that marked the critical popular press and often relying on limited data.

Moreover, much of the scholarship, like most of the popular reaction, seemed unaware of two questionable assumptions upon which it is based. First, scholars seemed to assume that whatever they studied was, in fact, Moral Majority rhetoric. Sermons, statements by conservatives from other organizations, religious fund-raising letters, and books published before the creation of the Moral Majority were all uncritically accepted as being illustrative of the organization's rhetoric.

Second, scholars seemed to assume that the Moral Majority was an unchanging monolith or, at least, that whatever changes occurred did not need to be discussed. They never asked whether the ideas propounded in 1979 were the same as those propounded in 1985 or whether the rhetorical strategies used in 1980 were the same as those used in 1985. This unspoken assumption of an unchanging monolith is surprising in view of what we know about social movement theory, which argues that movements tend to espouse radical positions early in their existence and to moderate those positions over time.[27]

These problems seemed to flow from several limitations in the research. In part, there is a degree of antipathy among academics to fundamentalists in general and to the Moral Majority in particular. This dislike made it difficult to present careful, balanced analyses. A greater difficulty, however, might have been the problems with gaining access to the necessary primary source materials.

SOURCE MATERIALS

There is a bewildering array of materials and representatives that have been associated, in some way, with the rhetoric of the Moral Majority. Isolating those materials that were most germane and most closely associated with the organization was difficult, in part because the organization of the Moral Majority was not well understood and in part because so many different materials were available. Hence, in order to make a valid judgment about what exactly constitutes the rhetoric of the Moral Majority, we first have to understand both the nature of the organization and the rhetorical genres involved.

The Organization of the Moral Majority

With offices in Washington, D.C., and Lynchburg, Virginia, the organization claimed 4 million members through much of 1983. This number rose, without explanation, to 7 million in the closing weeks of that year.[28] Even the estimate of 3 million seems wildly inflated given the fact that the Moral Majority's newspaper never reached more than 750,000 homes, its mass mailings went out to only 250,000 people, and its average mailing produced only about 10,000 contributions.[29] The Reverend Falwell too often boasted of his fund-raising prowess for us to believe that he would have consistently overlooked 96 percent of his potential contributors. Outsiders who tried to estimate the organization's membership, by giving Moral Majority the benefit of the doubt, still reached a membership of no higher than 800,000 at its peak. This dispute about simple facts will become a recurring theme.

The organization's Lynchburg headquarters were remarkably unprepossessing for a group that claimed to be reshaping America. The organization was housed in the upper two floors of a renovated paint warehouse in a decaying section of Lynchburg. The upper floor housed the editorial offices of the newspaper, the mass-mail computer room, a receptionist's office, and several modest executive offices. The building was furnished as simply as possible with light industrial carpet, small desks, and portable partitions for walls. There were many wall decorations; all of them were pictures of the Reverend Falwell standing with famous people. The lower floor housed machinery and a room of telephone operators. The street level, connected with Falwell's ministry, housed a used clothing store and food pantry. The Washington offices were similarly modest, but functional.

The Moral Majority claimed the existence of fifty independent state chapters. This claim created difficulties in determining the precise nature of the organization. First, only a handful of state organizations seemed to function independently, while the rest existed only on paper. These ghost chapters had public relations value, but added little else.[30] Second, the federalism of the organization, that is, the national organization with supposedly independent state organizations, created difficulties in determining who said what. Many of the most radical claims associated with the Moral Majority were made by people associated with the state chapters rather than with the national organization. These statements included claims that moral citizens should feel free to burn objectionable books, that homosexuality should be a capital crime, and that a bakery should be closed for selling obscene gingerbread people.[31] Indeed, the national office had periodically been embarrassed by such radical statements and, on occasion, had either denounced the speaker, repudiated the sentiment, or both. In one extreme case, the national office adopted the simple expedient of buying the state chapter from the holder of its incorporation papers and then dissolving the operation.[32]

Difficulties arise even when we concentrate exclusively on the national organization because, in fact, the national structure was comprised of a variety of separate but related institutions. The exact number of these organizations varied with the creation and dissolution of special "task forces," but there was always a core of four groups: (1) the Moral Majority, Inc., the parent body and source of frequent mass-mailed appeals; (2) the Moral Majority Foundation, a tax-exempt arm that published the *Moral Majority Report* and conducted voter education and registration drives; (3) the Moral Majority Legal Defense Fund, also tax-exempt, with a mission comparable to the liberal American Civil Liberties Union's; and (4) the Moral Majority Political Action Committee, which supported politically conservative candidates but which was largely inactive in the later years of the organization.

Unrelated to the Moral Majority, but inevitably confused with it, were Falwell's various ministries through the Thomas Road Baptist Church and the "Old-Time Gospel Hour." In addition to his role as a conservative politician, Falwell was also the director of a religious empire that received $100 million per year in contributions, and that encompassed the second largest church in the nation, a direct-mail operation so large that it had its own Zip Code, an active publishing house, and weekly religious broadcasts carried on more outlets than any other.[33] In this role, Falwell produced innumerable taped sermons and several books, all of which he claimed were unrelated to the political positions sponsored by the Moral Majority. Falwell contributed to the confusion by seldom identifying the persona in which he was speaking (i.e., as cleric, private citizen, or politician) but frequently issued ex post facto clarifications aimed at getting himself out of trouble.

In order to avoid the pitfalls of misattributing Falwell's personal convictions and statements to a political organization whose members might not share Falwell's religious credo, we need to focus our attention on those artifacts that were incontrovertibly associated with the Moral Majority. These public statements were issued primarily through the Moral Majority, Inc., and the Moral Majority Foundation, but also include several political interviews granted by Falwell.

Rhetorical Artifacts

Biweekly mass-mailed fund-raising letters were the most visible public statements by the Moral Majority. The letters were sent to an average of 250,000 households, and about 4 percent of the recipients responded to the average mailing. Generally, letters addressing national security issues produced much more money than those dealing with more traditional moral issues.[34] Virtually all of the organization's revenue was generated by these letters, but there is no reliable estimate of the amount raised. Some observers suggested that the organization raised $5.8 million in 1982, about twice their 1980 total, and over $7.2 million in 1984, but the sources of these estimates were not specified.

These letters, written by a consulting firm in Richmond, Virginia, were part of a highly stylized genre. All included an apocalyptic introduction; descriptions of ill, blame, and cure; a plan that generally entailed a symbolic reaffirmation through signing some petition or declaration and a financial commitment in the form of a donation; and a conclusion that placed the onus of salvation on the individual member. They were, in form, identical to the fund-raising letters of nearly every other political group in the country and seemed to produce rates of return comparable to those of other groups.[35]

The *Moral Majority Report* was a monthly newspaper that chronicled the organization's undertakings and provided other stories of interest to morally sensitive readers. The *Report*, which began publishing on March 14, 1980 (oddly enough, with the claim of being Volume One, Issue Three), absorbed the "Old-Time Gospel Hour's" *Journal-Champion* and adopted its reader-ship lists. The mailing list remained relatively stable with one-half to three-quarters of a million *Reports* delivered directly to homes and an additional quarter-million being distributed through conservative churches.

The *Report* dramatically changed both its physical appearance and editorial content over the six years of its existence. Three physical changes were apparent.[36] The length of the *Report* nearly doubled between 1980 and 1985, the layout of the front became clearer and more vivid, and the quality of the graphics improved markedly. Although any one of these changes might seem trivial, their net effect was to produce a *Report* that appeared ever more professionally produced and presentable.

The editorial changes were as striking, but we will need to save our detailed discussion of that for later chapters. We can say that, in general, the early editions of the *Report* were little more than a conglomeration of unrelated reprints and essays by conservatives not associated with the Moral Majority. There was essentially no writing by officers of the Moral Majority or by members of the *Report* staff. Christian athletes, conservative members of Congress, fundamentalist ministers, and assorted members of the New Right seem to have had articles included in the paper by virtue of mere availability. The few articles contributed by Moral Majority members tended to focus on issues of organizational mobilization, while the outsiders wrote about euthanasia, abortion, pornography, the defeminization of female soldiers, and forced sterilization. It took about two and a half years before staff-written articles consistently dominated the *Report*'s space. As the staff began to dominate the writing chores, the agenda of the newspaper became more dominated by reporting on significant events of the day and their relevance to the Moral Majority's mission, and less like an unrelated montage of politically correct essays.[37]

Finally, the Moral Majority produced a folded pamphlet entitled "What Is the Moral Majority?" This pamphlet remained virtually unchanged over the years. It described the goals and missions of the Moral Majority, and was the one item sent to every person who requested information about the Moral Majority. It is a good place to start our inquiry into the nature of the Moral Majority.

WHAT IS THE MORAL MAJORITY?

The Reverend Falwell answered the question "What is the Moral Majority?" in the pamphlet of the same name:

The answer is simple—Moral Majority, Inc., is made up of millions of Americans, including 72,000 ministers, priests, and rabbis, who are deeply concerned about the moral decline of our nation, and who are sick and tired of the way many amoral and secular humanists and other liberals are destroying the traditional family and the moral values on which our nation was built. We are Catholics, Jews, Protestants, Mormons, Fundamentalists—blacks and whites—farmers, housewives, businessmen. We are Americans from all walks of life united by one central concern—to serve as a special interest group providing a voice for a return to moral sanity in these United States of America.[38]

This definition provides several insights into the organization and its world. First, problems were defined in moral terms. The problem was "the moral decline of our nation" and the solution was "a return to moral sanity." For the Moral Majority, even problems that were normally considered to be economic or political in nature became moral problems. This moralism had a profound impact because fundamentalists see moral and immoral actions strictly in terms of individual choice. Thus, the Moral Majority was forced to find specific, concrete, culpable villains. Crime in the streets could not be caused by impersonal social forces; it could be caused by Ted Kennedy. The Moral Majority was comfortable finding individual villains, because this matched the beliefs of the conservative Christians who comprised the bulk of the organization's membership. Fundamentalists, for example, believe in Satan, a real, physical being who is personally the source of all evil.

The second thing we can draw from the definition was the Moral Majority's view of itself as a backlash against "many amoral and secular humanists and other liberals." The Moral Majority was needed because these groups were destroying the historic foundations of the nation. The Moral Majority objected to a lot of specific changes that had occurred since the 1960s. The exact list of indictments changed frequently, but most speakers agreed that the first great crime was the 1962 Supreme Court decision outlawing prayer in public schools. This is the starting point for Falwell's "seventeen years of liberal insensitivity" in the 1979 quotation appearing early in this chapter. These objectionable actions, the Moral Majority claimed, continued up to the present and variously included: the introduction of the Equal Rights Amendment, the Supreme Court decision legalizing abortion, the "pornography explosion," The Federal Communication Commission's application of the "Fairness Doctrine" to nasty remarks about homosexuals, and government attempts to interfere with the operation (and tax-exempt status) of church-run schools.[39] These claims clarified both the nature of the organization's foes and the group's ultimate mission of restoring what was, rather than seeking what might be. The notion of a return to an earlier, better time ran throughout the Moral Majority's rhetoric and provided a constant, reassuring touchstone both against the rapid, threatening changes they perceived in society and against attacks on the legitimacy of their actions.[40]

Third, the traditional family was singled out for particular attention, and the defense of the family served to energize the organization's most controversial positions. The Moral Majority, for example, opposed the women's movement and nontraditional roles for women, because both of these encouraged women to define themselves in primarily nonfamilial roles. Similarly, public tolerance of homosexuality was opposed because the Moral Majority assumed that sexual preference was a matter of choice and because such tolerance encouraged people to choose a life-style that precluded a family. Pornography was opposed, in part, because it glorified nonmarital sexuality, and because it encouraged acts (infidelity and violence) that undermined the stability of the family. Finally, stronger child-abuse laws, and shelters for victims of domestic violence were opposed for a hodge-podge of reasons: the centers served as places to receive antifamily indoctrination, the autonomy of the father would be unjustifiably questioned, and the likelihood of maintaining a family would be decreased as options increased. Again, the secular value, "the family," was intricately interwoven with the importance of the family in Christian religion, as when the relation of God to worshippers was described as that of father or husband to the family, and when God was described as "Our Father" and we were "His children."

Fourth, the group went to some trouble to divorce itself from the popular assumption that it was merely a fundamentalist fringe group. Falwell emphasized the religious diversity of the organization's membership, 30 percent of whom were Catholic, and, rather pointedly, listed "Fundamentalists" as the last religious affiliation. This was consistent with Falwell's position that Moral Majority was not a religious organization, although it was guided by God-given principles. Falwell's claim, and perhaps his dream, was that the Moral Majority was not the tool of any parochial group, but rather was an expression of the will of all sorts of moral Americans. Indeed, by early 1984, Falwell was even willing to admit to the presence of a few well-meaning agnostics in the organization.[41]

Finally, Falwell accepted the designation as "a special interest group." This seems strange, at first, since it seems to contradict the notions of universalism we just discussed. The contradiction here is more apparent than real. This label was first applied to the Moral Majority by its detractors, who were trying to make it appear small and petty. Falwell accepted this epithet in the same spirit that historically has led many outcast groups, such as the Quakers, Shakers, and Puritans, to turn the slurs against them into defiant symbols. Falwell, later in the pamphlet, carried this same notion of symbolic reversal a step farther by reveling in the fact that his organization was denied tax-exempt status: "Moral Majority, Inc. . . . does not give tax-deductible receipts for contributions. It is supported by Americans who are willing to invest in their country." This claim, then, indicted those who were unwilling to contribute without a corresponding tax deduction. They were slackers, unwilling to make the effort to "return this nation to the values and principles on which it was built." Although other insights could be mined from Falwell's definition, the broad vision of the organization is evident: it was moral Americans of all faiths banded together to oppose a liberally induced national decline with a strongly moralistic program. They were the moral majority.

The Moral Majority's Mission

We can turn our broad understanding into a much deeper one by looking at the way that the Moral Majority's representatives described its mission. They made the notion of "returning America to moral sanity" concrete through a series of lists. These lists range from Falwell's brief assertion that "we take a pro-life position . . . we are pro-family . . . we are pro-morality . . . above all, we are pro-American"[42] to much more extended explanations of key values. In "What Is the Moral Majority," Falwell explained:

Here is how Moral Majority, Inc., stands on today's vital issues:

1. we believe in the separation of church and state.

2. we are pro-life . . .

3. we are pro-traditional family . . .

4. we oppose the illegal drug trade in America . . .

5. we oppose pornography . . .

6. we support the state of Israel and the Jewish people everywhere . . .

7. we believe that a strong national defense is the best deterrent to war . . .

8. we support equal rights for women . . .

9. we believe the E.R.A. is the wrong vehicle with which to obtain equal rights for women . . .

10. we encourage our Moral Majority state organizations to be autonomous and indigenous.[43]

This list served to mask a number of specific positions held by the organization; for example, opposition to homosexuality was subsumed within support for the traditional family, support for capital punishment was a qualifier on their pro-life stance, and opposition to communism was a presupposition to their national-defense stance. In general, though, this was a conservative and pretty noncontroversial roster of objectives.

The list we just looked at presented the most public face of the Moral Majority, since it was in the organization's most public document. There were, however, other lists for other audiences. Subscribers to the *Moral Majority Report* (people who gave money to the Moral Majority) encountered another list: the "seven great principles" upon which America was built. Contrasting these lists may give us a sense of the difference between what the Moral Majority was to its members and what it wanted to be considered by everyone else.[44] In 1981, Falwell explained that:

without question, America is great because America was founded on seven basic principles derived from the Judeo-Christian ethic . . . they are . . .

1. the principle of the dignity of human life . . .

2. the principle of the traditional monogamous family . . .

3. the principle of common decency . . .

4. the principle of the work ethic . . .

5. the principle of the Abrahamic convenant [the notion that God treated a nation as it treated Israel] . . .

6. the principle of God-centered education . . .

7. the principle of divinely-appointed establishments . . .[45]

The contrasts between the lists are informative in this sense: the pamphlet, which was written for outsiders, was totally devoid of references to religion, God, and/or our Judeo-Christian heritage. In the pamphlet, the moral and political values were rooted in the American historical tradition. Falwell went so far as to argue that the organization was not religiously based, did not support "born-again" candidates, was not trying to gain theocratic power, and would oppose the rise of any "Ayatollah-type person." In contrast, "the seven great principles," which were contained in an article for Moral Majority members, were clearly identified as religious, and the Lord God was identified as the divine appointer of governments.

This difference in the rhetoric addressed to different audiences recurred throughout the work of the Majoritarians, who seemed to be struggling to balance the notion of a secular mission with their intense religious commitment. Indeed, this dichotomy haunted the organization until the end of its existence: the Moral Majority of 1985 was an extremely secular organization, trying to reach a mass audience and failing financially, while the rhetoric of the Liberty Federation of 1986 showed a sharp resurgence of references to the role of Christians in politics and of God in the future. The size of the subscriber lists between the *Moral Majority Report* and the *Liberty Report* is one interesting indicator of the difference between the two groups. In 1986, its first year of operation, the Liberty Federation used only about one-fifth of the subscriber list bequeathed to it from the Moral Majority. This was about the number of subscribers reached by the 1980 *Moral Majority Report*. There is a clear implication, which we will explore later, that the organization responded to its worst crisis of confidence by shedding much of its secular garb, and returned to the supporters and rhetoric upon which it was founded.

In sum, the Moral Majority imagined itself as being something special, as defending something truer and more lasting than the latest opinion poll results. Its critics were quick to point out, though, that the Moral Majority was not so much moral as moralistic. They found something painfully selective about a system that defined the Strategic Defense Initiative as a moral issue while choosing to ignore poverty and disease. The Moral Majority's distinctly pragmatic response to these criticisms was to claim that these excluded issues were divisive or unimportant to their constituency.[46]

Four Initial Characterizations

At any given moment, there were fifty or sixty organizations, state and federal, answering to the name "Moral Majority." As we have seen, these groups had little central coordination. This made for a lot of "rhetorics of the Moral Majority," but there was still a coherent core from which we can outline the basic character of the crusade. First, the crusade responded to liberal wrongs more strongly than to its own visions. This is seen in Falwell's claim that the organization was a response to seventeen years of liberal irresponsibility. It is also illustrated by the fact that all of Falwell's fund-raising letters stressed the need to respond to some new calamity (e.g., a Larry Flynt satire or weakening resolve in Central America) rather than the need to carry forward the positive aspects of the Moral Majority program.

Part of the reason for this reactiveness on the Moral Majority's part is simple: calamity "sells well." It is easy to get people worked up to deal with a crisis; it is difficult to move them with just a vision. So, Falwell found crises. Another reason is that, without a crisis, fundamentalists were not going to have any thing to do with politics or political groups. Historically, fundamentalists avoided politics like a plague. They were, by and large, poor, and the poor are not politically active. Moreover, fundamentalist preachers had, for decades, denounced involvement with the secular world.

Second, the organization was ardently Christian. Although it defined itself as a political organization welcoming all faiths, all of the organization's first generation of state chairmen and national spokesmen were fundamentalists. The organization did not deny that its directives were all Biblically derived, and it had been the object of charges of thinly masked anti-Semitism.[47] Of necessity, understanding the political rhetoric of the Moral Majority will require some understanding of its religious heritage. We will try that in the next chapter.

Third, the organization was preservationistic; that is, it looked to the past for an explanation of current troubles and for the right solutions to those troubles. In Falwell's book, *Listen, America!*, he systematically compared the debased present with a far better past. According to Falwell's book, such problems as the Civil War, the Great Depression, and World War II were basically inconsequential challenges to a then-godly nation.[48] This bias was consistent with what scholars have come to expect of conservative movements and is probably also consistent with the fundamentalist notion that we had entered a period of increasingly intense tribulation that served as a prelude to the Second Coming of the Messiah.[49]

Finally, the organization was simplistic; that is, it professed the belief that problems had single causes and simple solutions. Falwell highlighted this simplicity in a number of ways. He claimed, at the end of each fund-raising letter, that an individual contribution was enough to solve virtually any problem. He argued that "simplistic answers [occur when] you follow the proper equations and proper processes." He posited the simple act of prayer as the essence of any program of national salvation, and he rejected the notion that national problems were too complex for popular solutions.[50] As with the other characteristics, this one seemed consistent with the fundamentalist view of the world, which claimed one source of right, one source of wrong, one path to salvation, and one source of truth. In embracing the notion of literal inerrancy for the Bible and in rejecting metaphorical interpretation of The Word, the fundamentalists purposefully rejected complexity as a real concern.

These four characteristics were not merely sidelights to the political issues the organization confronted. Rather, they lay at the very heart of the organization's understanding of the issues that confronted it. They showed the Majoritarians how to interpret and solve these problems. As such, they were inconsistent with Falwell's oft-repeated assertions that the Moral Majority was nonreligious. They help us understand the constraints under which the organization's rhetors operated. Moral Majoritarians were constrained in their ability to adapt to new problems, and to alter their stated positions by their need to keep solutions simple and moralistic. Solutions that had not previously existed were rejected, and solutions that were merely politically expedient were detested.

This means that we should judge the significance of such policy changes that did occur against the standard of morally rigid fundamentalists and not against the ethical relativism of its liberal critics. When, for example, Falwell conceded that abortion should be permitted when the life of the mother was in danger but refused to condone abortion in the cases of rape and incest, we should recognize that this concession might have represented great personal, spiritual, or political risks, and might have been viewed by supporters as near heresy. Outsiders, unaccustomed to considering the importance of the organization's religious heritage, might undervalue or even denigrate these changes as representing minor repairs where wholesale reconstruction was needed. In context, however, these same changes might have represented a sincere striving to accommodate to a pluralistic political system that was both new and alien.

A RHETORICAL APPROACH TO THE MORAL MAJORITY

This book is an attempt to describe and interpret the ideas and strategies of the Moral Majority in as dispassionate a way as possible. Cognizant of the difficulties of identifying the rhetoric of the "mainstream" Moral Majority and the diffuseness of the organization, it is based on a relatively small set of publications that are clearly those of the Moral Majority—not unofficial pronouncements of some speaker who might or might not be representing the organization's perspective and not even the pronouncements of its leader, the Reverend Falwell, unless it was clear that Falwell was speaking as a Moral Majoritarian.

More specifically, this work is based on a complete set of the *Moral Majority Report.* The *Report* represented the only incontrovertible, publicly available source of information for the entire period of the organization's existence. Interviews with Falwell about his work with the Moral Majority, articles written by Moral Majority officials in "outside" publications, and the direct-mail letters were used as supplements whenever they added some perspective to the arguments raised in the *Report.*

Questions to Be Addressed

Our central question is, "How did the rhetoric of the Moral Majority change?" We know that the central allegation against the Moral Majority focused on its presumed inflexibility, rigidity, and anti-democratic tendencies. To a large degree, we can assess the degree of validity of this charge by looking at the ways in which the organization changed, the ways in which it resisted change, and the reasons underlying both.

There are three subsidiary questions that bear on the rhetoric of the Moral Majority. They are: (1) Why was the Moral Majority attacked so violently? (2) Was the Moral Majority a success or a failure? (3) Did the dialectic between the Moral Majority and its opponents shed any light on basic elements of the process of political change?

Working Theses

In answering these questions, this book will advance four major theses. The first is that the Moral Majority did not change its position on fundamental questions of philosophy or policy, but it did change its presentation of those arguments in an attempt to enhance the credibility of its position with a broader audience. This does not mean that the Moral Majority made purely cosmetic concessions. Rather, it fundamentally altered the means by which it pursued its ends. Specifically, the organization became less confrontational, more willing to engage in tactical concession, and more willing to embrace the norms of a pluralistic democracy. While these changes did not endear them to liberals or earn them the label of "politically moderate," it did earn them a greater degree of political legitimacy.

The second thesis is that the Moral Majority suffered remarkably high levels of exposure and vilification both because of its unique position and because of miscues by the organization. Historically, its ascendancy corresponded with the "conservative revolution" of the 1980 electoral campaign; the Moral Majority was chosen as a media symbol for a whole range of activities. The media often chooses a single individual or event to condense a much more complex phenomenon, because it is both easier and more dramatic to focus on a few concrete images rather than on abstract concepts. In this way, the organization became a lightning rod. This level of attention was heightened by a certain rhetorical insensitivity in the organization's history. The name "Moral Majority" seemed so presumptuous as to demand response. (The group's organizers were actually sensitive to this concern, and they considered more generic names such as "Coalition for the Future of America.") In addition, the Reverend Falwell was, by mere dint of being a fundamentalist minister, an affront to many in the media. Teresa Carpenter, a Pulitzer Prize-winning journalist, summed up the general reaction when she said that "when I step within a 10-foot radius of a fundamentalist minister, *my reason clouds over.*"[51] The combination of white socks with Brooks Brothers' suits, a Southern accent, and a considerable paunch made Falwell easy to caricature. A willingness on his part to blurt out ill-conceived ideas (e.g., that Hugh Hefner should be imprisoned, that God does not answer the prayers of Jews, and that the Devil concocted the idea of separating church and state) made such caricatures inevitable.

This second thesis does not deny the existence of reasoned responses to the Moral Majority. There were, as we noted in the literature review, many sensible people writing about the New Christian Right. What I am arguing is that the predominant public response was ad hominem and that the level of emotion engendered by the Moral Majority's position on any given issue was more intense than the emotions generated by responses to other people holding the same beliefs. So, for example, attacks on the Moral Majority's abortion position were more intense than attacks on the Catholic Church's, even though both organization defended the same ground.

The third thesis is that the organization was both a success and a failure. Although it is clear that the Moral Majority gained little by way of legislative victories and its members were repeatedly and soundly defeated each time they ran for public office, the organization helped to reshape the terms of public debate. By the late 1980s, public debate seemed to center on what sorts of controls should be imposed on pornography and abortion, rather than whether such controls should be imposed.

The question became how much the defense budget should grow not "should it grow?" In gaining these successes, however, the organization may have precipitated its own collapse by destroying the very sense of urgency that energized its early supporters and justified their financial sacrifices on behalf of the organization.

The fourth and final thesis is that the reception of the Moral Majority highlighted the difficulties of bringing new actors into the political system. The vilification of the Moral Majority and the often inaccurate portrayals of its policies by scholars, politicians, and the media seem to represent a recurring theme in American politics. These responses point out serious limits to the flexibility of the polity with regard to accepting the validity of new perspectives and demands.

PLAN OF THE BOOK

The above mentioned sources have been analyzed with a view to determining in what ways the Moral Majority's rhetoric changed. After sketching the history of the Moral Majority in Chapter 2, we will look at 1979-81, the tumultuous first three years of the organization's life, in Chapter 3. Chapter 4 will focus on consistency and change in the organization's later agenda. Chapter 5 will look at changes in its use of war imagery to describe the world. The sixth chapter will focus on the end of the Moral Majority and the rise of its successor, the Liberty Federation. At that point, we will also discuss the implications of the changes that occurred and that have failed to occur.

NOTES

1. Jeffrey Hadden, "Taking Stock of the New Christian Right," *Christianity Today*, 13 June 1986, p. 38.

2. "Falwell Attempts to Mend Inter-faith Fences," *Washington Post*, 4 April 1985. This article lacks a page number because it was obtained through the Moral Majority archives, whose clipping service does not save page numbers.

3. Statement of Jerry Falwell, *Congressional Record*, 25 February 1981, p. E704.

4. "Falwell Forming Group to Look at Broad Issues," *New York Times*, 4 January 1986, p. 6.

5. Quoted in Jeffrey Hadden and Charles Swann, *Prime-Time Preachers* (Reading, MA: Addison-Wesley, 1981), p. 149.

6. Ibid., pp. 149-150.

7. Parren Mitchell, "Unjustified Arrogance by the Moral Majority," *Congressional Record*, 5 December 1980, p. E5311.

8. John Jenkins, "Toward the Anti-Humanist New Christian Nation," *The Humanist*, July-August 1981, p. 22.

9. Arthur Ide, *Tomorrow's Tyrants* (Tucson: Monument Press, 1985).

10. A. Bartlett Giamatti, "The Moral Majority Is a Threat to the Freedom of Americans," excerpts from the address, *Pittsburgh Post-Gazette*, 5 September 1981, p. 8.

11. William F. Buckley, Jr., "The President of Yale versus the Moral Majority," *Pittsburgh Post-Gazette*, 5 September 1981, p. 9.

12. Anthony Lewis, "William Buckley Misread the Message of the Book of Jonah," *Pittsburgh Post-Gazette*, 11 September 1981, p. 11.

13. Quoted in Hadden and Swann, *Prime-Time*, p. 149.

14. Barry Goldwater, "Excerpts from Goldwater Remarks on Rightists," *New York Times*, 16 September 1981, p. B9.

15. Ibid., p. B9.

16. Jerry Falwell, "Falwell Answers Goldwater," *Human Events*, 10 October 1981, p. 22; John Lofton, "Goldwater versus Goldwater: Which Should I Believe?" *Human Events*, 17 October 1981, p. 6; "Goldwater Dismays Conservatives—Again," *Human Events*, 20 January 1982, p. 14.

17. James D. Hunter, "The Liberal Reaction," in *The New Christian Right*, Robert Liebman and Robert Wuthnow, eds. (Hawthorne, NY: Aldine Publishing, 1983), pp. 150-166; Daniel Maguire, "Conclusion: On a Note of Hope," *The New Subversives* (New York: Continuum, 1982); "Lear TV Ads to Oppose Moral Majority," *New York Times* 25 June 1981, p. C13.

18. Perry Young, *God's Bullies* (New York: Harper, Row & Winston, 1982); Phillip Finch, *God, Guts and Guns* (New York: Seaview Press, 1983); Flo Conway and Jim Siegelman, *Holy Terror* (New York: Dell, 1984).

19. Maguire, *New Subversives*, p. 137.

20. John Cooper, "Book Review: *The New Subversives*," *Christian Century*, 2 March 1983, p. 192.

21. Patricia Pingry, *Jerry Falwell: Man of Vision* (Milwaukee: Ideals Publishing, 1980); Richard A. Vigeurie, *The New Right: We're Ready to*

Lead (Falls Church, VA: The Vigeurie Co., 1980); Burton Pines, *Back to Basics* (Washington, DC: The Heritage Foundation, 1982); William Willoughby, *Does America Need the Moral Majority?* (South Plainfield, NJ: Bridge Publishing, 1981); Dinesh D'Souza, *Falwell: Before the Millennium* (Lake Bluff, IL: Regnery-Gateway, 1984).

22. Willoughby, *Does America*, pp. 10-11.

23. D'Souza, *Falwell*, p. 23.

24. Daniel Yankelovich, "Moral Majority Expresses Concerns of Millions of Worried Parents," *Conservative Digest*, March 1982, pp. 8-10; John Kater, *Christians on the Right* (Minneapolis: Winston Press, 1982), pp. 2-3.

25. David Nyhan, "The Conservative Crusade," *Boston Sunday Globe Magazine*, 3 May 1981, p. 12ff; "Split-Up Evangelicals," *Newsweek*, 26 April 1982, pp. 88-91; Martin Marty, "Precursors of the Moral Majority," *American Heritage*, February/March 1982, p. 99; Martin Marty, "A Christian View of the Moral Majority," *Across the Board*, April 1981, p. 7; Frances Fitzgerald, "A Disciplined, Charging Army," *The New Yorker*, 18 May 1981, p. 62ff.

26. The two journal articles on the Moral Majority were, Charles Conrad, "The Rhetoric of the Moral Majority: An Analysis of Romantic Form," *Quarterly Journal of Speech*, 69 (May 1983): 159-170 and A.L. Zimmerman, "Thunder Everywhere: The Developing Rhetoric of Jerry Falwell," *Speaker and Gavel* 19 (1981-1982): pp. 22-28. In chronological order, the dissertations included: Roy E. Buckelew, "The Political Preaching of Jerry Falwell: A Rhetorical Analysis of the Political Preaching of Rev. Jerry Falwell in Behalf of the Moral Majority During the 1980 Political Campaign," diss., University of Southern California, 1983; Douglas F. Brenner, "The Rhetoric of the Moral Majority: Transforming Perceptions of Opposition," diss., University of Nebraska-Lincoln, 1984; Patricia A. Jefferson, " Spokesmen for a Holy Cause: A Rhetorical Examination of Selected Leaders of the New Religious-Political Right," diss., Indiana University, 1984; Vernon O. Ray, "Rhetorical Analysis of the Political Preaching of the Reverend Jerry Falwell: The Moral Majority Sermons, 1979," diss., Louisiana State University, 1985; and, Kim S. Phipps, "The Rhetoric of the Moral Majority Movement: A Case Study and Reassessment of the Rhetoric of Conservative Resistance," diss., Kent State University, 1985. Representative of the approach of many convention presentations was Daniel Hahn, "The Paranoid Style of the Moral Majority," New York, 1981 (mimeographed). Professor Hahn presented essentially identical papers to the Eastern Communication Association and the New York State Communication Association Conventions, but was unable to supply exact dates for either. Other disciplines were not greatly active in

examining the Moral Majority's strategies. For example, Liebman and Wuthnow's *The New Christian Right* is the most complete sociological analysis presently available, yet it contains only two short sections in one of twelve chapters on symbolic issues.

27. Herbert Simons, "Requirements, Problems and Strategies: A Theory of Persuasion for Social Movements," *Quarterly Journal of Speech*, 56 (February 1970): 1-11.

28. "Falwell: A Winner of Hearts," This article was mailed by the Moral Majority in 1983 in response to a request for information concerning the organization's founding. It is a newspaper article that contains no identifying information and that did not discuss the organization's origins.

29. Interview with Ted Derrick, administrative editor, *Moral Majority Report*, Lynchburg, VA, 24 May 1985.

30. James Guth, "The New Christian Right," in Liebman and Wuthnow, *New Christian Right*, p. 33.

31. Jerry Falwell, "An Interview with the Lone Ranger of American Fundamentalism," *Christianity Today*, 4 September 1981, pp. 22-23; Willoughby, *Does America*, pp. 44-45; Michael Lienesch, "Right-Wing Religion: Christian Conservatism as a Political Movement," *Political Science Quarterly*, 97 (Fall 1982): 417-418.

32. "Fore 'Going Back to Preach Gospel,'" *New York Times*, 2 December 1981, p. B2.

33. Interview with Russell File, Liberty University archivist, Lynchburg, VA, 25 May 1985; "The Rise of the Falwell Empire," *Washington Post*, 25 September 1984, p. D9; William R. Goodman and James J.H. Price, "Life with Falwell," *Penthouse*, May 1983, p. 80ff.

34. Derrick interview.

35. Roger Craver, "Launching an Effective Fundraising Effort," *Campaigns & Elections*, Spring 1985, pp. 56-59; Larry J. Sabato, "Mailing for Dollars," *Psychology Today*, October 1984, pp. 38-43; Tina Rosenberg, "Diminishing Returns: The False Promise of Direct Mail," *Washington Monthly*, June 1983, pp. 32-38.

36. The *Report* dramatically changed both its physical appearance and editorial content over the six years of its existence. Three physical changes were apparent. First, the length of the *Report* grew. From March 1980 through December 1983, the *Report* was sixteen pages long; from January 1984 through April 1985, twenty pages; and from May 1985 through December 1985, twenty-eight pages. Second, the design of the front page changed. From March 1980 through September 1983, the front page was dominated by a single large picture or drawing with a list of article titles along one margin. From October 1983 through April 1985, pictures were nearly squeezed off the front page as columns of

text and various headlines gave the *Report* a more newspaper-like appearance. In May of 1985, the *Report* reverted to a tabloid format, with the front page again dominated by a single large, four-color illustration and marginal story titles. Third and last, the quality of the graphics improved markedly. The early *Reports* were distinctly inferior to most high school newspapers. They were printed in black and white, the occasional attempts at red and blue embellishment were muddy and poorly aligned, and the photographs tended to be grainy head-and-shoulders shots of the main character or author of each story. Beginning in early 1983, the graphics improved with the advent of blacker ink and focused photographs. The most startling change occurred in May 1985, when the newspaper adopted a tabloid format required by its new printer, which also printed the venerable *Grit*. The pages were reduced by about 15 percent, the print size was reduced about 20 percent, and sharp, four-color graphics were introduced. Although any one of these changes mnight seem trivial, their net effect was to produce a *Report* that appeared more professionally produced and presentable.

37. The first issue of the *Moral Majority Report* clearly dominated by staff work did not appear until October of 1983.

38. Jerry Falwell, "What Is the Moral Majority," 1980, n.p.

39. Fitzgerald, "Charging Army,"pp. 120, 122.

40. Marian Christy, "Reverend Jerry Falwell: Fire and Ice," *Boston Sunday Globe Magazine*, 1 November 1981, p. A29.

41. Letter from Cal Thomas, Moral Majority vice-president for communications, 13 January 1984.

42. "Enforcing God's Law in the Voting Booth," *The Humanist*, March/April 1981, p. 6.

43. "What Is the Moral Majority?"

44. Which we can infer from the fact that the *Moral Majority Report* was received only by members of the organization, while the pamphlet was sent to outsiders curious about the Moral Majority.

45. Jerry Falwell, "America Founded on Seven Great Principles," *Moral Majority Report*, 18 May 1981, p. 8.

46. "Lone Ranger" interview, p. 26; Lienesch, "Right-Wing Religion," p. 419; Dudley Clendinen, "Christian New Right's Rush to Power," *New York Times*, 18 August 1980, p. B7.

47. One example of these fairly common accusations would be the chapter "Jewish Indiscretions," in William Goodman and James Price, *Jerry Falwell: An Unauthorized Profile* (Lynchburg, VA: Paris and Associates, 1981), pp. 1-14.

48. Jerry Falwell, *Listen, America!* (New York: Doubleday, 1980), p. 9.

49. Martin Marty, "Insiders Look at Fundamentalism," *Christian Century*, 18 November 1981, p. 1196.

50. Sashti Brata and Andrew Duncan, "Interview with the Reverend Jerry Falwell," *Penthouse*, March 1981, pp. 152, 154.

51. Quoted in Hadden and Swann, *Prime-Time*, p. 168.

Chapter Two

Genesis of the Moral Majority

In 1607 Puritans established the first settlement in this country at Jamestown.

For about [its first] 180 years, this country without any question was the leading world power in every area . . .

I have read about the War Between the States; indeed that was a perilous time. No one questioned the fact, however, that our nation would survive that time.

Jerry Falwell, 1980[1]

These are people more interested in making history than in studying or preserving it.

Russell File, Liberty University archivist, 24 May 1985[2]

The leaders of the Moral Majority never seemed to reflect upon their own history, frequently changed those claims they were willing to make, and were unresponsive to requests for information about the founding of the organization and the sources of its inspiration.[3]

Nonetheless, the Moral Majority was so rooted in the past that we cannot ignore its history. In this chapter, we will look at five related topics: the members of the Moral Majority; the history of American fundamentalism; the history of the New Christian Right; the life of Jerry Falwell; and the founding of the Moral

Majority. First, we will take a brief look at the membership of the Moral Majority in order to get some sense of their values and concerns. Second, we will examine the history of the fundamentalist movement in America. Third, we will examine the history of a contemporary movement referred to as "the New Christian Right." Fourth, we will present a brief biography of the organization's founder, Jerry Falwell. Fifth, we will look at the founding of the Moral Majority, with special attention given to the variant accounts of its formation. Each of these undertakings will entail specific historiographic problems, which we will discuss within the appropriate sections.

THE MORAL MAJORITARIANS

The Moral Majoritarians were "cultural fundamentalists." While this particular phrase was used by only one scholar,[4] the notions it embodied were widely shared by commentators on the organization. The word "cultural" served two functions: first, it directed our attention to those issues that predominated in the organization. The Moral Majority was concerned primarily with those topics that influenced how the historic American culture had been created and preserved. The Moral Majority sometimes discussed America's political, economic, diplomatic, and religious heritages, but it looked at these issues only when, and as, they related to the family and other domestic institutions. So, for example, America's religious heritage interested the Moral Majoritarians only in so far as it helped understand how better to protect the family and familial values. Second, "cultural" indicated the source of the organization's inspiration: America. There was no notion supported by the organization that either transcended or superseded those ideas that the organization inherited from nineteenth-century America. Despite the best efforts of detractors to depict the organization as some alien, fascist force and of apologists to claim a new vision for America,[5] the reality was that the organization's leaders were unimaginative and pragmatic while its followers were typical lower middle-class citizens primarily concerned for the welfare of their children. For both of these groups, leaders and followers, what "should be" was largely derived from what "was." That is, they were both seeking a relatively nonradical defense of a historic culture.

In this way, the Moral Majoritarians espoused a form of civil religion. By civil religion, we mean more than just national self-worship, jingoism, or patriotism. Civil religion, in addition to a veneration of this nation, also involves "the subordination of the nation to ethical principles that transcend it and in terms of which it should be judged."[6] Civil religion thus imparts an aura of the sacred throughout the secular realm.

Underlying America's civil religion was the notion that America was the redeemer nation and Americans were a chosen people. "Implicit in this notion is the belief in a messianic universal mission, a sort of sacred nationalism that connects manifest destiny with universal ideals."[7] The idea of civil religion tied together these religious concepts with faith in economic growth, individuality, and prosperity, since each of these things helped to strengthen the nation (and, thus, works God's will).

Civil religion did not, however, grant America a free ride to greatness. There was a corresponding assumption that America accepted certain Biblical moral imperatives in return for its greatness. Hence, Puritanic traditions of fidelity, sobriety, charity, and honesty must be honored for the nation to fulfill its ordained role.[8] As long as we remained moral, we remained prosperous and free; if we sank into immorality, collapse and conquest followed.

The available social studies showed that the Moral Majoritarians fit well into this framework of beliefs. Frances Fitzgerald's sympathetic appraisal of Moral Majority's supporters was based on extended observations in Lynchburg and with missionaries in New York City. She concluded that she was dealing with "the kings and queens of the covered-dish dinner" set who were determined to hold onto their precarious gains, which might be a new Chevy or the ability to take the family for a week's vacation to the shore, while not becoming seduced by the hedonistic world beyond them. This meant that military service was still a norm and college education, except for Bible colleges, an exception. While they were supposed to believe, as a matter of faith, that they should avoid "the world," it did not quite work out that way in practice. In discussing their pastor's condemnation of "the world," Fitzgerald noted that:

The world in this context [means] pornography, drugs, "secular humanism," and so on: the evils of the world as they see them, and not American life in general . . . their prescriptions for life look very much like tactics for integrating people into society rather than tactics for separating them.[9]

Operating from a broader base of research, Donna Day-Lower surveyed several studies and concluded that "The American Dream" bound together the diverse groups in the Moral Majority: they were either living out the Dream and wanted to protect their gains or they had failed to achieve it, but desperately hoped to do so. This latter group especially opposed changes that threatened to mutate the Dream before they ever had a chance to achieve it.[10] Finally, an extensive survey of Moral Majority supporters in the Dallas-Fort Worth area showed that they were neither very bigoted (they were more anti-Catholic, anti-Semitic, and racist than the general population but not overwhelmingly so) nor, in many ways, very conservative. The survey found, for instance, that the followers were much more liberal with regard to abortion, sex education, separation of church and state, the Equal Rights Amendment, and values clarification in schools than were their supposed leaders. The authors of the Fort-Worth study concluded: "The defense of a cherished lifestyle from the perceived ill effects of secularization and a wish to correct the failures of modernity present a plausible framework for understanding the goals of the New Christian Right."[11] The appeal of the Moral Majority to the vast bulk of its supporters, then, lies not with crusades against a secularized anti-Christ so much as with Falwell's promise of "a return to normalcy."[12]

THE FUNDAMENTALIST TRADITION

The normalcy to which these good people aspired was a legacy of their Puritan forebears. The Puritans left Europe in the 1620s and 1630s in order to escape the apostacy of a doomed church and the degeneracy of a secular society. They believed that America was a special land that had been reserved for them (e.g., hidden from the Spaniards) by a special act of Providence. This land was preserved for these latter-day Israelites so that they might carry out an important commission: to found a Christian commonwealth that lived in perfect conformity with scriptural dictates and served as a kingdom of Heaven on Earth. Ultimately, this little kingdom would complete the Lord's work begun by the Reformation and would serve as a beacon to the degenerate.

In order to light this beacon, however, the Puritans had to live within the confines of their stringent ethic, which claimed that "people would be honest, love one another, be loyal to the community, help the poor, work hard, remain true to God, pray, read the Bible and avoid scandalous conduct such as swearing, whoring and drinking excessively."[13] These were, of course, the same values that lay at the heart of America's civil religion. The Puritans made contributions to three broad areas of American values. First, they helped set the norms of private conduct through the teachings that we identify with the Puritan ethic. Second, they helped define the relationship between the individual and the state by teaching both respect for authority (since government was a God-given institution) and the need to distrust authority (since government was constituted of the "children of Adam"—a horribly sinful lot). Third, they helped to define the relationship between the covenanted community and the outer world, which was embodied in the notion that "the saved" had an ordained mission to spread their life-style and beliefs among a world filled with the unsaved. In sum, these were a striving people who tended to make righteous and often apocalyptic judgments about the world around them.[14]

While the Puritan church did not survive through the succeeding centuries, its heritage to the Protestant denominations did. The Protestant mainstream remained dominant and largely united for over two centuries, until the pressures of an increasingly modern world triggered a schism in the late nineteenth century. The fundamentalists were one product of this schism. The success of Protestantism in dealing with the challenges of the seventeenth, eighteenth, and early nineteenth centuries allowed it to remain relatively unified.

By the middle of the nineteenth century, a number of profound changes were shaking the Protestant world. A sharp upswing in immigration brought unprecedented numbers of Jewish and Catholic immigrants to America. More disturbing than the sheer numbers of immigrants was the fact that many were from southern and eastern Europe, and their physical differences from the northern European made them a visible intrusion. With the advent of the industrial revolution, the urban population burgeoned, and many people abandoned their agrarian life-styles. Subsequently, cities became identified as hotbeds of corruption, misery, decay, and degeneration. Many city-dwellers yearned for the lost innocence and bucolic rightness of rural life but had become economically bound to the city. The teachings of Darwinian scientists raised doubts about the Biblical account of creation. Biblical authority was further undermined, if only in limited circles, by the advent of "higher criticism," which inquired into the words and sources of the Scriptures. The upshot of these inquiries was the suggestion that much of the Bible was more metaphorical than literal and that it might actually be just the writings of very holy men who were limited by their cultures, rather than the Word of God.

While much of the Protestant establishment was able to reconcile itself to these changes, a substantial minority opposed them vigorously and publicly for three decades. These theologians operated out of a pietistic revivalist tradition and, over the three decades between 1890 and 1920, spawned three parallel movements in response to these modernist heresies. All of these movements claimed common antecedents, and all claimed to accept the same fundaments of faith, but the very elements of their faith drove them apart. One movement was referred to as "the holiness revival," which stressed a dramatic "second blessing" and a subsequent life of perfect holiness, which they referred to as "complete sanctification." The Church of God, the Nazarenes, and the Salvation Army were representative of the sects within this movement.

The second movement was pentecostalism, which shared many of the attributes of the holiness movement, but which added a stress on supernatural powers, speaking in tongues, and faith healing. The penetecostals ultimately decided that speaking in tongues was the single, definitive sign of rebirth in the Holy Spirit.

The third movement was fundamentalism. There is no definitive account of the early years of fundamentalism, in part because historians have tended to have little interest in religious history and in part because the movement existed thirty years before the label "fundamentalism" came to give it some coherence. We can, nevertheless, draw an outline of fundamentalist history based largely on the works of Calvin College historian George M. Marsden.[15] Fundamentalism began to emerge, with the holiness revival and pentecostalism, in the late nineteenth century. Its intellectual base was largely urban and northern, although its popular support would always be greatest in the southern "Bible Belt" states. Fundamentalism first appeared in a series of premillennial prophetic conferences that argued for a literal interpretation of an inerrant Bible. The term, "fundamentalist," derived from a series of twelve booklets published between 1910 and 1915; these booklets, in the words of Harvard theologian Harvey Cox, "delineated what their writers believed were the irreducible doctrines of the faith, the beliefs without which Christianity could no longer be called Christianity. These fundamentals of faith included belief in the deity of Christ, the Virgin Birth, the bodily Resurrection of Christ, the imminent Second Coming, the substitutionary atonement, and—very emphatically—the verbal inspiration and inerrancy of the whole Bible."[16] While fundamentalism started in the northern Presbyterian and Baptist denominations, its greatest effect was in energizing the nondenominational, revivalist churches of the South.

Until the 1920s, fundamentalism's antipathy toward the modern world was kept largely in check. By the 1920s, however, fears engendered by renewed immigration, the disrepute of much liberal doctrine in the wake of World War I, a perception of increasing moral laxity in the secular world that was evidenced by the rise of the cinema and jazz music, and the spread of evolution teachings all encouraged the re-emergence of fundamentalism. Fears of an immigrant wave and immorality heightened sympathy for the fundamentalist message, the decline of liberalism helped discredit fundamentalism's liberal antagonist, and the Scopes trial provided a focus for national attention.

These conditions were, however, more the exception than the rule. While fundamentalism did not die with Bryan in Dayton, it did renew its commitment to separatism after the Scopes fiasco and effectively vanished. The doctrine of separating from a doomed world, augmented by the ridicule they suffered in the course of the Scopes trial, convinced the fundamentalists to establish separate schools, separate colleges, separate churches, separate denominations, and a largely separate life-style that eschewed political contacts.

Since virtually every commentator traces the roots of funda-mentalists to this period,[17] we need a careful catalogue of their contributons to the psyche of their modern brethren. First, the fundamentalists were militantly antimodern. They did not like modern society, modern ideas, or modern learning. The irasci-ble Billy Sunday summarized their general view when he pro-claimed, ''Thousands of college graduates are going as fast as they can straight to hell. If I had a million dollars, I'd give $999,999 to the church and $1 to education.''[18] Fundamentalists cherished the inerrant Word of God, the simple solutions of Biblical teaching, and the eternal verities of Light versus Darkness.[19] In order to insure the promulgation of their truths, the fundamentalists established a series of Bible colleges with which to train a new generation of leaders, and from which Falwell and many of his associates have graduated.[20]

Second, fundamentalists generally embraced the notion of premillennial dispensationalism, which taught that the world was, quite literally, going to hell as a result of Satan's efforts. As the world reached the nadir of depravity, the Lord of Hosts would return and lead an army of the saved and angels against the anti-Christ. A thousand-year reign of peace would be followed by an apocalyptic struggle and the end of time. While many predecessor sects, including the Puritans, had embraced a similar theology, the fundamentalists made it the centerpiece of their belief and the chief explanatory device against the entire secular world.

Finally, the fundamentalists practiced a form of free-enterprise preaching, in which the preacher held absolute authority; if parishioners did not like his preaching, they were free to leave. These highly authoritarian preachers were neither answerable to their parishioners nor to any denominational hierarchy, and they never developed the sort of reserve, intro- spection, or tact that accountability might entail. In addition, these preachers brought the authoritative Word of God, which taught that leaders (God, the preacher, and the father, in their respective realms) were to be followed rather than questioned. In short, fundamentalists distrusted the secular world as Satan's domain and placed great reliance on the unquestioned word of poorly educated, intolerant preachers to deliver the Lord's eternal message.[21]

We must not, however, be deluded into accepting this greatly simplified account as a definitive or controlling statement about the Moral Majority's world view. What we are trying to do is un- derstand the major forces behind the way the organization under- stood its environment. While these broad-stroke murals certain- ly help us to see the highlights, we will gravely misunderstand the Moral Majority if we read them too literally. First, the Moral Majority was not the Puritans, and it was not the fundamenta- lists of the last century. The Moral Majority would countenance less church-state interaction than the Puritans, but more than the fundamentalists. The Moral Majority had less reverence for reason than the Puritans, but more than the fundamentalists. Moreover, the Moral Majority professed a greater tolerance for dissent and a more ecumenical approach to religion than either of its antecedents.

Second, the Moral Majority was not just the offspring of either or both of these groups. Even though its leaders were drawn from a fairly narrow political and religious spectrum, neither the leaders nor the members were able to wholly divorce them- selves from the influences of the secular, pluralistic world about them. As a result, the organization showed a greater range of ideas than we would expect of a purely fundamentalist group. As historian George Marsden argued:

we find in current fundamentalism the amalgamation of a fascinating variety of traditions. Some are highly intellectual and some highly emotional, some elitist establishmentarian and some directed toward outsiders, some concerned with public policy and some privatistic, and all are mixed with various American assumptions and folklore. During the twentieth century these were fused together, trans-formed and sometimes fragmented by intense efforts simultaneously to fight American secularists and to convert them. The result is a movement fraught with paradoxes that have made it sociologically mystifying.[22]

This confusion was heightened by a second dividing of the Protestant community, when in 1941 and 1942 the fundamentalists split into two factions around the issue of separation. The most militantly separatist fundamentalists, often affiliated with the American Council of Christian Churches, continued to preach absolute separation in the pursuit of salvation. Other fundamentalists, however, felt called upon to witness (i.e., to evangelize) to the world. Known as the "evangelicals" or the "neo-evangelicals," these fundamentalists were associated with the National Association of Evangelicals and might be described as the Billy Graham wing of the party. Somewhat more moderate and somewhat more intellectual than their separatist brethren, the evangelicals spread from their traditional homelands to try to bring the message of salvation to the masses. The politics in this wing of fundamentalism ranged from the liberation theologists of the far left to the traditionally anticommunist followers of the Reverend Graham on the right. So, then, we may view the Moral Majority as being descended from these intellectual traditions, but we must avoid mistaking influences on the Moral Majority for a definitive description of their minds.

THE NEW CHRISTIAN RIGHT

The Moral Majority was a subset of a larger movement, which we will call the New Christian Right.[23] The New Christian Right may be defined as all of those organizations that were striving to reorder the American polity to make it more nearly conform with a Biblically inspired order. This would include such organizations as the Religious Roundtable, the Christian Voice, and the Moral Majority, but would exclude more secular organizations such as the National Conservative Political Action Committee, the Conservative Caucus, and the Conservative Victory Fund. While some portions of the legislative agenda overlapped, the secular New Right had a distinct organizational and intellectual history, and espoused many causes excluded from the New Christian Right agenda (e.g., the Panama Canal, gun control, and tax reform). Similarly, the New Christian Right would exclude those organizations of the far right (such as the John Birch Society and the Christian Anti-Communist Crusade) that were so obsessed with conspiratorial fantasies that they had abandoned political action in favor of preparing for the communist/satanic apocalypse.

This leaves a broad spectrum of organizations that shared a number of beliefs. Synoptically, most held that America had a special mission in the world and that it could be returned to a commitment to that mission. Unfortunately, to their minds, the proper order of things in America had been grievously disrupted: the proper roles of men and women were awry, Christians found themselves excluded from the polity they had established, the state had usurped many of the roles of the family (as witnessed by sex education, values clarification, child abuse legislation, and so on), and respect for the historic order of things was missing. While the commitment to conspiratorial interpretations was varied between groups, most professed to see the world in nativist and Manichean terms. This meant that they tended to polarize issues into black versus white, Christian versus satanic, and millennial versus apocalyptic, but they also tended to depict their opponents as representing the extremes of their various affiliations. As a result, all feminists became lesbians or, better yet, radical feminist lesbians, all socialists became communists, all humanists became atheists, and so on.[24]

Two types of events seemed responsible for the emergence of the New Christian Right. One type of event shall be called "facilitative"; these were events that made it possible for Christians (a term that the fundamentalists restrict to themselves) to become involved in politics. The facilitative events included the participation of liberal clerics in the civil rights and antiwar movements of the 1960s and early 1970s; even though the New Christian Right clergy was not supportive of this

involvement at the time, the actions of people such as the
Reverend Martin Luther King, Jr., and the Reverend Daniel Ber-
rigan helped to convince the public that churches had a legitimate place in politics. The election of Jimmy Carter to the presidency also facilitated fundamentalist involvement in politics
by placing a born-again Christian into the highest elected office
in the land. Further, the emergence of new high-technology
operations made the Right's computer-driven fund-raising
possible, and the creation of the secular New Right provided
role models and technical assistance to the Christian Right.[25]

A second type of event can be called "trigger events"; they
made it necessary for Christians to become active. In times past,
a number of challenges brought Christian activists swarming
over their wall of separation; these issues included the abolition
of slavery, Prohibition, unrestrained immigration, the candi-
dacy of Al Smith, a Democratic Catholic for president, and the
threat of communism.[26] In the case of the New Christian Right,
their general dislike of liberal society was piqued by a number of
specific actions. The primary affront was the 1962 Supreme
Court cases banning prayer in the public schools, which was
frightening both because the case was won by an atheist and
because of the threat it represented to the welfare of their
children. The New Christian Right was also irritated by the 1973
Supreme Court case legalizing abortion, IRS inquiries into the
discriminatory practices of fundamentalist schools, FCC
inquiries into the operation of the television ministries, the
panoply of other groups demanding gay, black, and women's
liberation, and the FCC's application of the "fairness doctrine"
to remarks about gays.[27] While the specific issues are doubtless
different for each group (and, for Falwell, while the list changes
across time[28]), we can see two distinct categories of triggers: some
issues describe particularly obnoxious conditions in society,
such as abortion and prayerless schools, while others represent
direct assaults on the Christians' separate society. This category
would include the various FCC and IRS rulings on fundamentalist schools and broadcasts. When asked why fundamentalists
launched their holy war on secular society, one activist offered a
very straightforward explanation; "Because we were attacked
first, that's why!"[29]

There were three major organizations that dominated the

New Christian Right: Christian Voice, the Religious Round-table, and the Moral Majority. Christian Voice, the oldest of the organizations, was founded in January 1979 by California minis-ters Richard Zone and Robert Grant.[30] The Christian Voice was actually a coalition of several smaller, antigay, antiporno-graphy, pro-family groups on the West Coast. In 1979, it opened a Washington office and solicited endorsements of New Right legislators, such as Senators Gordon Humphrey, Roger Jepsen, and Orrin Hatch. In 1980, the Voice made headlines with its endorsements of specific candidates, its infamous Morality Re-port Cards on legislators, and its tactic of mailing complete campaign strategies to assorted electoral challengers. The Voice parlayed the early support of the Christian Broadcasting Net-work, which gave them exposure on over 100 stations, and technological sophistication into a high-visibility role. They gained this visibility despite a membership of only 150,000, which was far short of their goal of 1 million members and of the Moral Majority's claim of 4 million members.

The Religious Roundtable was formed in September 1979 as a way of reaching those clergymen who might be uncomfortable with the high profile of the Christian Voice and the mass orientation of the Moral Majority.[31] Founded by Southern Baptist minister and Conservative Caucus organizer Ed McAteer, the Roundtable specialized in reaching conservative ministers, who were still nominally in the Protestant main-stream, through a series of mailings and conferences that were designed to help them better understand political issues and activism. The most famous of these conferences was the National Affairs Briefing in Dallas during August 1980. The Briefing attracted thousands of conservatives[32] and was addressed by every major figure in the New Right, including Jerry Falwell, James Robison, Pat Robertson, Ronald Reagan, Phyllis Schlafly, Paul Weyrich, Howard Phillips, and Timothy LaHaye.[33] This was the same event at which candidate Reagan admitted that "I know you cannot endorse me, but I want you to know that I endorse you!" Unlike other organizations, the Roundtable did not seek to achieve mass mobilization, and rather modestly, claimed to have reached 40,000 people between the Briefing and the November election.

Before looking at the last organization in our trio, the Moral

Majority, it will be useful to look at the life of the man who brought it into existence.[34]

JERRY FALWELL

Several generations of the Falwell family have lived in Lynchburg, Virginia. Jerry Falwell's grandfather, Charles Falwell, was a dairy farmer whose family lived in the hills east of Lynchburg and who had farmed the narrow valleys since the mid-1800s. With the industrialization of Lynchburg in the early twentieth century, the town grew in the direction of the Falwell home, and their area eventually became part of the Fairview Heights section of Lynchburg. Fairview Heights was a poor and rough area with no street lights, no running water, no paved roads, and no law enforcement. During the Prohibition era, the area was controlled by gangs of bootleggers, and the more respectable citizens of Lynchburg frightened their children with tales of vice and white slavery in Fairview.

Falwell's father, Carey, was the oldest in a family of boys. He was a shrewd but poorly educated man who managed a succession of enterprises: bootlegging, a service station, an oil dealership, and a small trucking operation. In the early 1930s, Carey went into business for himself and owned a dance hall, restaurant, and "tourist court." The family was doing well enough that they bought a house in the fashionable Rivermont section and had it moved, piece by piece, to Fairview Heights. Carey Falwell's fortunes quickly soured in the Depression, though; he killed his brother in self-defense in the midst of a heated business argument in 1931, went bankrupt in 1933, had to sell his businesses to another brother, and began drinking heavily. Through hard work, Carey Falwell regained a degree of prosperity but was never able to control his alcoholism. In 1948, when Jerry Falwell was fifteen, Carey died of cirrhosis of the liver.

Jerry Layman Falwell was one of four Falwell children who survived infancy. Falwell and his twin brother, Gene, were younger by more than a decade than their brother and sister. Apparently, Falwell's birth was not planned. While Jerry Falwell was an extremely intelligent, ambitious, and aggressive youth, his brother Gene was friendly and easygoing. Gene ended up being an unchurched agnostic who ran a local trailer court. Jerry's older brother, Lewis, ran an excavation company in the Lynchburg area. Falwell's sister, Virginia, ran the family businesses after Carey's death, was a Justice of the Peace for a while, worked in her husband's Hilltop Restaurant, and worked for Falwell's ministries.

Falwell was born on August 11, 1933. During his early life, Falwell (like his grandfather, father, and brothers) had no use for religion, although his mother was a strict fundamentalist. Jerry attended public school and was an outstanding student: he finished second in the state spelling championships and graduated with a 98.6 average. Falwell also possessed a photographic memory, and was a skilled and competitive athlete who, as a senior, captained a high school football team.

Throughout his youth, Falwell was rambunctious. Even Falwell's "official" biographers go into great detail on Falwell's ill-spent youth. We are told that Jerry was a leader of the local youth and that he often provoked fights with gangs from neighboring areas by having the smallest member of his group pick a fight; as soon as the fight began, Falwell and the remainder of his crew would crash out from ambush to attack. Most accounts of his life also mention that he once set a snake loose in a classroom, hid a live rat in a teacher's desk, tied up a gym teacher and locked him in the school basement, pulled the steering wheel off a car that was moving at sixty miles per hour, and piled peoples' porch furniture on their roofs. At least one source noted that, as a Halloween prank, Falwell dragged a railroad tie onto the street near his home and set it ablaze. The heat was so intense that the asphalt road caught on fire, and the Lynchburg Fire Department had to be dispatched. Falwell's more sympathetic biographers also mention that he was denied the opportunity to deliver his high school's valedictory address because he had been suspended for "a prank." Only the more critical writers note that the "prank" was handing out cafeteria passes to other members of the football team, which the school considered stealing.

In 1950, Falwell enrolled at Lynchburg College with the intention of transferring to Virginia Polytech after his sophomore year to pursue a degree in mechanical engineering. Instead, Falwell completed his sophomore year in good standing, had the highest math average at the college, and transferred to an obscure, unaccredited Baptist college in Springfield, Missouri.

As Fitzgerald noted, "just how he came to this decision was not clear."[35] Falwell was not a pious person, and he had every reason to expect a successful and lucrative career as an engineer. Yet he forsook that for the alien and uncertain future of a Bible preacher. Falwell claimed that he and a friend, Jim Moon, went to the Park Avenue Baptist Church to try to arrange dates with two attractive young ladies, the organist and pianist. Falwell and Moon did, subsequently, marry these two young ladies. According to Falwell, something touched his heart during the service, and he answered an altar call. After counseling by a youth minister, Falwell spent months studying the Bible and felt a calling to the ministry.

Falwell studied at the Baptist Bible College from 1952-53, where he proved that his conversion had not dampened his spirits. In one episode, Falwell flooded a neighbor's dorm room with a hose, and after the neighbor had cleaned up the mess, Falwell arrived to dump an additonal five gallons on the floor. In another, he rode his motorcycle through the dormitory's hallways. Also while at college, he pursued his roommate's fiancee, in part, by ripping up love letters that his roommate had asked him to mail.

Falwell greatly admired the men he met at the Baptist Bible College, for many of them ministered to congregations of thousands. Falwell resolved to build such a congregation for himself. Falwell's eldest son, Jerry, Jr., noted that, "Fundamentalism appealed to my father because of the entrepreneurial nature of it. The idea is to build a big church, build a big school, start a TV ministry. Most religions are not like that."[36] Falwell first demonstrated his entrepreneurial ability when he inherited a Sunday school class. After some weeks, Falwell still had only one student, and the superintendent threatened to cancel the class. Falwell immediately began canvassing local playgrounds and parks, looking for eleven-year-olds to recruit. By the time the school year was over in May, Falwell had assembled a class of fifty-six students.

Falwell took the 1954 school year off to work at the Park

Avenue Baptist Church in Lynchburg and graduated from college in 1956. He returned to Lynchburg, exploited a schism at the Park Avenue Baptist Church, and departed with thirty-five dissidents to found his own Thomas Road Baptist Church. The first services were held in a converted Donald Duck bottling plant in June of 1956; parishioners had to spend two days scrubbing residual cola syrup from the place before services could be held. By November, the congregation constructed a separate building in which to worship. Through the practice of "saturation evangelism," that is, door-to-door visits by Falwell to every family within miles, Falwell increased the congregation from 35 to 854 within a year.

The growth of Falwell's empire was remarkable. His sermons were broadcast on local radio within a week of the congregation's founding. He aired television specials within eighteen months. By 1964, Thomas Road underwent a major expansion through the construction of an 800-person auditorium; six years later, a 3,600-person auditorium was added. All through this period, Falwell continued his saturation evangelism: he published leaflets and a weekly newspaper, the *Journal-Champion*; by 1967, his "Old-Time Gospel Hour" aired weekly on local television; he established attendance by others; and he began offering his weekly sermons for sale as audio-cassettes.

The 1970s was a decade of continued growth and occasional crises. Falwell introduced various high-tech elements, such as color TV cameras, a national network, and computers for targeting his mass-mailed appeals for funds. His congregation grew to around 18,000 members and he claimed a television-radio audience of 25 million, and later 50 million. These latter figures were widely disputed, with the Arbitron and Neilsen audience surveys placing his total audience at no more than 1 million, with that number falling after his entry into politics.[37]

At the same time, Falwell was repeatedly embroiled in legal and financial crises. The Securities and Exchange Commission brought a suit against Falwell for an unsecured bond offering, which was later settled out of court. As part of the settlement, the ministry spent four years under the financial control of a group of responsible local businessmen in return for an SEC promise to drop the phrase "fraud and deceit" from its complaint. In 1979, Falwell transferred the health insurance policies for his employees to a Texas-based "Christian" company, which went bankrupt within a year, was unlicensed, had assets of $128, and had unpaid claims of almost $300,000. Finally, Falwell was embarrassed by the "Menge affair." F. William Menge was a con artist, masquerading as a Christian business-man who managed to strike up a friendship with Falwell. Menge arranged a $500,000 loan for the church, traveled to the Middle East with Falwell, and then used his connections with the church to arrange $9 million in loans on which he defaulted. By 1980, Menge, once a member of the Gospel Hour board, was no longer on speaking terms with Falwell. In September of 1980, Menge was decapitated after falling from his riding mower. While the coroner ruled that Menge's death was accidental, at least one journalistic investigator suggested otherwise.[38]

The Thomas Road empire was rounded out by a seminary, a private Christian academy that was originally founded as a segregation academy (a claim Falwell vigorously denied), and a rapidly growing college. Falwell's announced intention was to expand his 5,000-person school into a 50,000-person university. In an interesting choice of words, Falwell has variously described Liberty University as a Christian equivalent to Notre Dame and a fundamentalist Harvard.

Over this whole period, Falwell's preaching became increas-ingly political. While his 1965 "Preachers and Politics" sermon denounced political activity by ministers, he later repudiated the sermon as "false prophecy" and had freely interjected a range of conservative political observations into his preaching.

Despite weekly death threats, Falwell's home life appeared placid. In interviews, his children spoke lovingly of their father and noted that his fundamentalist rectitude did not extend to child-rearing. He allowed his daughter, Jennie, to go on single dates at the age of fourteen and did not object to his children's interest in rock music, although he did preach against such music. Falwell's oldest son, Jerry, Jr., did not have to attend church as a youth, got into the University of Virginia law school on the recommendation of Senator Edward Kennedy, and claimed that his college friends tended to be Catholic and Jewish liberals.

We can make several concluding observations about the Reverend Falwell. First, he was driven. He was intensely competitive as a youth, and displayed unending energy in creating and sustaining one of America's largest churches and more lucrative television ministries. This was evidenced as much by his sports achievements and his dedication to his Sunday school class in college as by the later success of his ministry. Second, he was more strategist than tactician. Falwell seemed to have a good sense of where he wanted his ministry to go and the energy to drive it, but insufficient business acumen to sustain it. This was evidenced by his perpetual debt and his difficulty in realizing his goals within the time frames he set; for example, expansion of Liberty University was repeatedly halted by financial shortfalls, and its glory was more on paper than in fact. Third, Falwell was not nice to those he did not love. He has publicly derided his church choir for ineptitude, has twice raced his car toward a hapless security guard who had to dive out of the way, made vindictive asides about opponents during his broadcasts, and still revels in nasty college pranks. This may just reflect temporary setbacks in Falwell's struggle against the devil within himself, since he has also had many admirers who spoke of his charity and compassion. Regardless, there is a distinct dark side to Falwell that must have colored his decisions. Finally, Falwell's rhetoric was basically pedestrian. He was willing to admit that preaching was not his forte, and one did not need to listen to many broadcasts to reach the same conclusion: his messages showed no great insight into either the Bible or the human soul, his wording was uninspired and often clichéd, and his visible emotions ran a gamut from mildly interested to flatly pedantic. Whatever success Falwell had came through his considerable energy, good marketing, and sophisticated use of communications technology.

FOUNDING THE MORAL MAJORITY: VARIANT VERSIONS

The Moral Majority was incorporated in June of 1979 with the aim of mobilizing a great mass of disaffected conservatives. With a membership of between 250,000 and 8 million and with name recognition from about half of the American population,[39] the Moral Majority was the most controversial of the New Christian Right groups. We have, in the present chapter, already examined the organization and mission of the Moral Majority. We now need to look to its history.

Virtually the entire subject of the Moral Majority's history is surrounded by controversy and contradiction. A number of examples can be marshalled to illustrate this problem. The most accepted story of its origins is that a number of secular New Right leaders, such as Howard Phillips, Richard Viguerie, Ed McAteer, and Paul Weyrich, held a series of meetings in 1978 and 1979 with television evangelists to encourage their entry into politics. In particular, they supposedly courted Falwell for two years before a culminating nine-hour meeting in March of 1979. Contrarily, Falwell's staff held that the organization was a matter of his personal inspiration and that he rarely met with any political figures. In his autobiography, Falwell claims to have called this meeting himself, in May of 1979.[40] Concerning the organization's name, one version held that it was inspired by Howard Phillips's comment to the effect that "there is a great moral majority out there just waiting for a leader." At one point, Falwell claimed that the name came to him in a moment of personal reflection, and at another he attributed it to Weyrich.[41]

We noted earlier that the particular issues that sparked the formation of the Moral Majority were unclear; in addition, the spark that set Falwell into action is also unclear. One version held that he became involved as a result of New Right recruitment, while he once said that he was haunted by his young son's bedtime question, "Why don't you *do* something about it, Dad?"[42] Concerning the Moral Majority's program for America, one version held that the platform was strategically designed to avoid dissension among the various factions within the Moral Majority. Falwell both affirmed and denied this explanation of the platform. Concerning the organization's legal incorporation, one version held that the incorporation papers were prepared on the day after the March 1979 meeting by lawyers for the Conservative Caucus. Other accounts claimed that the papers were not drawn for three months and implied that they were prepared by Falwell's attorneys.[43] Concerning Falwell's advisers, one version claimed that former Representative Robert Bauman of Maryland, who had been convicted of sodomy with a minor, led a group that formulated many of Falwell's positions. Falwell claimed that Bauman had no input and had never served in any official capacity with the organization.[44] Even on the matter of Falwell's selection, there was some dispute about whether Falwell was a plum sought after by secular organizers or whether he was merely what they had to settle for after being turned down by more desirable candidates.[45]

We are safer in believing the various outsider accounts of the founding of the organization, at least until substantial proof to the contrary can be generated. This is because Falwell's interpretation of events was generally unsubstantiated, implausible, and self-serving. These suspicions were buttressed by observed incidents of mendacity on Falwell's part, and by the opinions of some scholars that the experience of off-the-cuff or "inspired" preaching led some preachers to view the truth as fluid and facts as malleable.[46]

If we choose to accept the outsiders' accounts of the Moral Majority's history, then we can construct the following general outline. Secular elements of the New Right, notably Viguerie, were baptized into national politics during Barry Goldwater's unsuccessful 1964 presidential campaign. Over the next decade, they grew progressively disillusioned by the major political parties because of their refusal to budge from the middle of the road. Consequently, these people began forming political organizations independent of the parties, and used these organizations to raise money for ideologically committed candidates and to educate a grassroots cadre into conservative political action. The reforms of the Federal Election Campaign Act (1971) and the Supreme Court decision in *Buckley v. Valeo* (1976) placed a premium on independent political activity, that is, those activities that were not explicitly tied to a national party or a particular candidate's campaign. As a result, the size and number of conservative political action committees grew.

By 1976, Viguerie and his associates suspected that they could reach a great untapped reservoir of funding and electoral support if they could gain the support of conservative Christians. At about the same time, the Reverend Falwell had embarked on a nationwide tour in conjunction with the Bicentennial celebrations. Falwell held rallies in dozens of urban stadiums, gained contacts with fundamentalists from across the country, and participated in antihomosexual legislative campaigns in Florida and California. Through Robert Billings, a conservative activist and former president of a fundamentalist college, New Right organizers, including Viguerie, contacted Falwell in 1977 and asked him to head a Christian political action organization. Unsure of its prospects, Falwell declined. Through the next two years, the secular elements continued to approach television evangelists and convinced a number to found political organizations. By January of 1979, Falwell began to respond positively to New Right contacts, and a high-level meeting was arranged for the spring. At this meeting, the broad elements of the Moral Majority's strategy, constituency, and organization were outlined, with experienced organizers from the New Right taking the chief role.

Over the next three months, plans were laid, contacts with other Christian organizations were strengthened, and a nationwide set of rallies sponsored by the "Old-Time Gospel Hour" were begun. By June, the role of secular leaders was ebbing as Falwell, an outstanding organizer, took greater operational control. In a series of letters and sermons in July of 1979, Falwell announced the formation of the Moral Majority, and enlisted the support of his congregation and viewers. Over the next half-year, Falwell barnstormed America, using the "I Love America" rallies to garner publicity and to cultivate leadership for the state Moral Majorities. By December, the national apparatus was in place, and Falwell claimed to have between forty-seven and fifty state chapters, though critics claimed that only eighteen were in actual operation.

The rhetoric of the Moral Majority was more than the sum of its historical legacies: neither the Puritan mind nor the fundamentalist heart, neither the organizations of the New Christian Right nor the experiences of a life preaching the Gospel completely defined it. This rhetoric both suspected and revered learning. It was missionary and capitalistic. It was intolerant and pragmatic. It was a complex amalgam that simultaneously spoke to the inevitability of sin and the necessity of salvation, and to

America's special destiny as well as its depraved nature. Yet this rhetoric is still a product of audience and circumstance as much as history and biography. The first great test of the Moral Majority's ability to reconcile these conflicts and unify its rhetoric came in 1979, with the beginning of a thirty-month drive to mobilize and legitimate this movement.

NOTES

1. Jerry Falwell, *Listen, America* (New York: Doubleday, 1980).

2. Interview with Russell File, Liberty University archivist, Lynchburg, VA, 25 May 1985.

3. These conclusions were based on three sets of observations. Statements about the variant versions of reality concerning the organization's history were substantiated at the end of chapter 2 and were drawn from the various published accounts of the organization's founding. Second, the unresponsiveness of the organization's functionaries to requests concerning the past was demonstrated in an exchange of personal correspondence and telephone conversations with the office of the vice-president for communications of the Moral Majority. While the vice-president's aide, Janet Buffington, was pleasant and forthright, she professed ignorance on questions of history, and while she very graciously sent an interesting array of material on a variety of subjects, none of the material concerned the organization's background. This was contrary to her assurances that such material was available and would be sent. Third, the organization refused to release much of their material to their own archives at Liberty University. Not only did the archive lack such material as copies of correspondence or the minutes of various meetings, it also did not have copies of the organization's mass-mailed appeals. As a result of this reticence and chronic underfunding, the archive remained mainly a collection of articles from a clipping service and back issues of the *Moral Majority Report* stored in a mountain of plain boxes in a five foot square cubicle.

It may be that the organization simply did not value accounts of its history, as the epigram from Mr. File suggested. This would then suggest that Ms. Buffington was simply in error about the availability of such documents. Alternately, this may have been a strategic posture that reflected the organization's desire to discourage unauthorized inquiries into its past. Such reticence might be explained by the organization's fear that inconsistencies in various accounts might be circulated or that early ideas might be publicized to the detriment of the movement's current effectiveness. In a 1985 interview, Ted Derrick, an editor of the *Moral Majority Report*, suggesterd that the organization's reluctance to release mass-mailed information represented the fear that competing organizations might learn the secrets of successful fund-raising by induction and, indirectly, injure the Moral Majority. This concern seemed far-fetched.

In any case, the available accounts of the organization's history drew heavily on the testimony of those currently outside of the Moral Majority and/or are simply asserted by the authors. These assertions may be based on comments from insiders who stipulated that they remain anonymous.

4. Joseph Tamney and Stephen Johnson, "The Moral Majority in Middletown," *Journal for the Scientific Study of Religion* 22 (June 1983): 145-157.

5. These efforts were described at the beginning of Chapter 1.

6. Robert Bellah, "Civil Religion in America," in *Beyond Belief* (New York: Harper & Row, 1970), p. 171.

7. Dick Anthony and Thomas Robbins, " Spiritual Innovations and the Crisis of American Civil Religion," in *Religion and America*, Mary Douglas and Steven Tipton, eds. (Boston: Beacon Press, 1983), p. 230.

8. Anthony and Robbins, *Religion and America*, p. 231.

9. Frances Fitzgerald, "A Disciplined, Charging Army," *The New Yorker*, 18 May 1981, p. 74.

10. Donna Day-Lower, "Who Is the Moral Majority? A Composite Profile," *Union Seminary Quarterly Review*, 37 (1983), 346-347.

11. These are the findings of the, so-called, Dallas-Fort Worth study. The complete study was published as: Anson Shupe and William Stacey, *Born-Again Politics* (New York: Edward Mellen Press, 1982). A summary essay by the authors appeared as "The Moral Majority Constituency," in *The New Christian Right*, Robert Liebman and Robert Wuthnow, eds. (Hawthorne, NY: Aldine Publishing, 1983), pp. 104-117. A brief synopsis can be found in Day-Lower, "Who Is," pp. 342-344. This study was very important, since it was the only published work to go beyond the organization's claim of what its membership believed and to survey the opinions of the mass membership.

The disjunction between claim and reality was, on some issues, very great. This might be partly explained by Shupe and Stacey's dependence on a surrogate population. That is, they did not interview card-carrying Moral Majority members per se; they interviewed people who had the demographic characteristics of Moral Majority members. Presumably, some fraction of this group were active members of the organization, but that assumption is unproven.

12. Jerry Falwell, quoted in Marian Christy, "Reverend Jerry Falwell:

Fire and Ice," *Boston Sunday Globe Magazine*, 1 November 1981, p. A32.

13. Ronald Reid, "Samuel Danforth, Errand into the Wilderness, *Commentary*," in "Anthology of Rhetorical Discourses in American History from the Colonial Era to the Civil War," Amherst, Mass., no date, p. 1.

14. There was a rich literature on the contributions of the Puritans to American culture. Some of the more recent works included: Gustav Blanke, "Puritan Contributions to the Rhetoric of America's World Mission," in *Studies in New England Puritanism*, W. Herget, ed. (New York: Peter Lang, 1983), pp. 199-232; Michael Lienesch, "The Role of Political Millennialism in Early American Nationalism," *Western Political Quarterly*, 36 (1983), 445-465; Ernest L. Tuveson, *Redeemer Nation: The Idea of America's Millennial role* (Chicago: University of Chicago Press, 1968); John Adair, *Founding Fathers: The Puritans in England and America* (London: J. M. Dent, 1982); and Sacvan Bercovitch, *The American Jeremiad* (Madison: University of Wisconsin Press, 1978).

15. George M. Marsden, *Fundamentalism and American Culture: The Shaping of Twentieth-Century Fundamentalism, 1870-1925* (New York: Oxford University Press, 1980). A synopsis of Marsden's work is: George M. Marsden, "Preachers of Paradox: The New Religious Right in Historical Perspective," in *Religion and America*, pp. 150-168. Reviewers have unanimously praised Marsden's interpretations, and his work is now among the most widely quoted in the area.

16. Harvey Cox, *Religion in the Secular City* (New York: Simon and Schuster, 1984), p. 44.

17. For example: David Harrell, "The Roots of the Moral Majority: Fundamentalism Revisited," *Occasional Papers*, Institute for Ecumenical and Cultural Research, May 1981; Ralph Chandler, "Worshipping a Past That Never Was," *Christianity and Crisis*, 15 February 1982, pp. 20-26; Charles Lippy, "The Development of America's Sense of Mission," in *The Apocalyptic Vision in America*, Lois Zamora, ed. (Bowling Green, OH: Bowling Green University Popular Press, 1982), pp. 52-55; Richard Pierard, "The New Religious Right: A Formidable Force in American Politics," *Choice*, March 1982, pp. 864-866; Michael Lienesch, "Right-Wing Politics: Christian Conservatism as a Political Movement," *Political Science Quarterly*, 97 (Fall 1982), 407; and Mel Piehl, "Reinterpreting the Fundamentalists: A Review Essay," *The Cresset*, April 1982, p. 15.

18. William McLoughlin, *Billy Sunday Was His Real Name* (Chicago: University of Chicago Press, 1955), p. 132.

19. Pierard, "New Religious Right," p. 864; Piehl, "Reinterpreting," p. 17; Marsden, "Preachers," p. 163.

20. "The Right's New Bogyman," *Newsweek*, 6 July 1981, p. 50.

21. This moderately demeaning description of the preachers' intellectual capacities and training seems to be widely shared, but does not apply to all fundamentalist preachers. Gresham Machen, one of the founders of fundamentalism, is recognized as being an exception. Moreover, Marsden tried hard to rehabilitate the intellectual respectability of the early fundamentalists by claiming that they were intelligent, reasonable men who merely rejected the dominant scientific paradigm of the day in favor of a more Baconian view of science. Marsden, "Preachers," pp. 162-165. Piehl, in his review essay, took sharp exception to this view, and claimed that the fundamentalists were adhering only to the outward appearances of rationality and that they espoused views of science that had been obsolete since before Newton. Piehl, ("Reinterpreting," pp. 18-20).

The classic rendering of the fundamentalists as anti-intellectual is Richard Hofstadter, *Anti-Intellectualism in American Life* (New York: Vintage Press, 1963). There is strong evidence that the fundamentalists were largely anti-intellectual and demonstrably undereducated. The Reverend Falwell showed much of the same suspiciousness in his preaching and his college. For instance, Falwell has instructed his parishioners to avoid reading anything other than the Bible and a few approved works. Fitzgerald, "Charging Army," p. 99. Similarly, he founded a college that, for a long while, had no library. The library was added only when an accrediting commission demanded one. Fitzgerald, "Charging Army," pp. 100-103. The textbooks used at Liberty University appeared, in 1985, to flow exclusively from small Christian publishing houses and tended to focus on simplified presentations of official versions of reality. Finally, the Reverend Falwell admitted that he viewed "academic freedom" as being the freedom to teach what one is told to teach. His institution grants no tenure in order to maintain control over the ideas advanced in its classrooms. Fitzerald, "Charging Army," pp. 100-101. As late as 1986, Falwell refused to transfer a thousand acres of land to the University's name, in part because the land would have given the University a potential independent source of income. This would have weakened the church's control over the university, which would have been bad because, as Falwell warned, "any college without a firm hand on the wheel drifts left."

Falwell's own education is spotty. His undergraduate degree is from an unaccredited college, and his "doctorates" are all honorary degrees from similar institutions. William Goodman and James Price, *Jerry Falwell: An Unauthorized Profile* (Lynchburg, VA: Paris and Associates, 1981), pp. ii-iii. Many of his admirers bask in Falwell's erudition; D'Souza approvingly noted that Falwell liked to quote Plato and Burke. Dinesh D'Souza, *Falwell: Before the Millennium* (Lake Bluff, IL: Regnery-

Gateway, 1984), p. 179. Nevertheless, Falwell's book is a mishmash of historical and logical error that is not attributable to simple carelessness. Robert M. Brown, "Listen, Jerry Falwell! A Response to 'Listen, America!'" *Christianity and Crisis*, 22 December 1980, pp. 360-364; Stanley Grenz, "Listen, America! A Theological and Ethical Assessment," *Foundations* 25 (April-June, 1982), 188-198. The compendium of historically inaccurate statements from Falwell in this chapter's epigram is typical of the claims he advanced in the book.

22. Marsden, "Preachers," p. 151.

23. The conglomeration was also referred to as: the New Religious Right, the New Religious-Political Right, the Christian New Right, and Born-Again Politics. The New Christian Right seemed most accepted, accurate, and simple.

24. Samuel Hill and Dennis Owen, *The New Religious-Political Right in America* (Nashville: Abingdon Press, 1982), p. 118; D'Souza, *Falwell*, p. 109.

25. Robert Zwier, *Born-Again Politics* (Downers Grove, IL: Inter-varsity Press, 1982), pp. 27-34.

26. Fitzgerald, "Charging Army," p. 111.

27. Ibid., pp. 120-122; Zwier, *Born-Again*, pp. 23-27; Hill and Owen, *New Religious-Political*, pp. 117-140; Robert Webber, *The Moral Majority: Right or Wrong?* (Westchester, IL: Good News Publishing, 1981), p. 25.

28. Fitzgerald, "Charging Army," p. 121.

29. Interview with Ted Derrick, administrative editor, *Moral Majority Report*, Lynchburg, VA, 25 May 1985.

30. Hill and Owen, *New Religious-Political*, pp. 57-62; James Guth, "The New Christian Right," in *The New Christian Right*, pp. 31-32. Perry Young, *God's Bullies* (New York: Harper, Row & Winston, 1982), pp. 101-105; Jeffrey Hadden and Charles Swann, *Prime-Time Preachers* (Reading, Mass: Addison-Wesley, 1981), pp. 139-140.

31. Hill and Owen, *New Religious-Political*, pp. 69-72; Guth, "New Christian," p. 33; Young, *Bullies*, pp. 121-122; Hadden and Swann, *Prime-Time*, pp. 137-139.

32. The official version of the Briefing's attendance is that 15,000 clergymen attended; it appears, however, that only about 2,500 of the attendees were members of the clergy. The remainder were lay people rushed in at the last minute to avoid the spectacle of the New Christian Right awash in a sea of empty chairs. Jeffrey Hadden, "Born-Again Politics: The Dallas-Briefing," *Presbyterian Outlook* 20 October 1980, pp. 5-6. In addition, 400 journalists were present.

33. Some of these names may be unfamiliar. Robison was a national television evangelist and vice-president of the Religious Roundtable. Pat Robertson was a Yale Law School graduate and founder of the

Christian Broadcasting Network. Phyllis Schlafly is most famous for her activities in opposition to the Equal Rights Amendment and is president of Eagle Forum. Paul Weyrich is founder of a New Right group, the Committee for the Survival of a Free Congress. Howard Phillips is founder of the Conservative Caucus and former director, during the Nixon administration, of the Office of Economic Opportunity. The Reverend LaHaye is a co-founder of the Moral Majority, and author of a series of books and articles alleging the presence of a secular humanist conspiracy to control the world.

34. This section draws from Falwell's autobiography, *Strength for the Journey* (New York: Pocket Books, 1987) and a number of previously cited works. These include Fitzgerald, D'Souza, Goodman and Price, and Webber. Additional biographic details come from: Myra McPherson, "Falwell: The Genesis and Gospel of the Reverend of the Right," *Washington Post*, 26 September 1984, pp. D1, D9; Erling Jorstad, *The Politics of Moralism* (Minneapolis: Augsburg, 1981), pp. 46-51; Patricia Pingry, *Jerry Falwell: Man of Vision* (Milwaukee: Ideals Publishing, 1980); Jerry Strober and Ruth McClellan, *The Jerry Falwell Story* (New York: Ibex Publishing, 1982); and Patricia Ann Jefferson, "Spokesmen for a Holy Cause: A Rhetorical Examination of the New Religious Political Right" diss., Indiana University, 1984, pp. 156-158. More scurrilous accounts include: L.J. Davis and Ernest Volkman, "If a Businessman Is to Be Judged by the Company He Keeps, Then Jerry Falwell May Have a Lot of Explaining to Do," *Penthouse*, November 1981, p. 63ff; L. J. Davis and Ernest Volkman, "Jerry Falwell, Part II, The Prophet Motive," *Penthouse*, December 1981, p 65ff; and, L. J. Davis, "Onward, Christian Soldiers!" *Penthouse*, February 1981, p. 52ff.

35. Fitzgerald, "Charging Army," p. 82.

36. McPherson, "The Genesis and Gospel," p. D9.

37. Associated Press, "T.V.'s Top Ten Evangelism Shows Register Decline in Audiences," *Pittsburgh Post-Gazette*, 27 November 1981, p. 31 and Chandler, "Worshipping a Past," p. 23.

38. Davis and Volkman, "If a Businessman."

39. Robert Liebman, "Mobilizing the Moral Majority," in *The New Christian Right*, p. 54.

40. Fitzgerald, "Charging Army," p. 124; Goodman and Price, *An Unauthorized*, p. 31; Falwell, *Listen, America*, 343.

41. Young, *Bullies*, p. 121; Pingry, *Man of Vision*, p. 69.

42. Fitzgerald, p. 120; Pingry, *Man of Vision*, p. 70.

43, Jerry Falwell, "An Interview with the Lone Ranger of Fundamentalism," *Christianity Today*, 4 September 1981, p. 26; Young, *Bullies*, p. 121; Hadden and Swann, *Prime-Time*, p. 136.

44. Goodman and Price, *An Unauthorized*, p. 27.

45. Day-Lower, "Who Is," p. 338.

46. These suggestions were raised in a conversation with Michael Casey, a doctoral candidate at the University of Pittsburgh, instructor at the University of Maine, and a fundamentalist. He suggested that parishioners did not demand consistency from their clergy, because they were primarily concerned with the inspiration that flowed in the course of an extemporaneous sermon.

Chapter Three

The Rhetoric of Mobilization and Legitimation, 1979–1981

We may be a silent majority now . . . [but] as the ranks of our Moral Majority swell into an army, we will be able to look at the politicians eye ball to eye ball [sic] . . . but if we are to succeed, we must demonstrate swift and radical reaction against the forces of evil working in our society. It is time to put our lives, our fortunes, our reputations—everything on the line—for this great nation of ours.

Jerry Falwell, August 1979[1]

The Moral Majority existed for its issues. Unlike other political organizations, the Moral Majority did not endorse candidates or supply money to campaigns; it did not issue "report cards" or supply expert advice on how to get elected. Rather, it existed to educate people about issues of importance, and to influence the legislative process by registering conservative voters and lobbying legislators. In order for the Moral Majority to press its agenda effectively, it needed to gain credibility as a political force. In the next two chapters, we will look at how the Moral Majority accomplished these two goals: Chapter 3 will focus on how the organization mobilized its consitituency and legitimized its role in politics, and Chapter 4 will focus on how it presented its agenda and how that agenda changed over time. By and large, these two goals were pursued at different times. The effort to legitimize the Moral Majority was the main theme of its first two and a half years of existence, while its legislative agenda dominated the next four years.

Although 1979, 1980, and 1981 saw the rhetors of a quickly maturing Moral Majority stress very different issues, for all three years their concerns centered more on the requisites of empire-building and establishing a place in the political system than on any particular set of substantive concerns. This claim will be developed into six sections: first, an examination of the fundamentalist doctrine of separation; second, a look at Falwell's "I Love America" rallies in 1979; third, a look at attempts in 1980 to mobilize supporters of the Moral Majority; fourth, a brief recapitulation of the criticisms of the Moral Majority that emerged in the mass media in 1981; fifth, an examination of the Moral Majority's tactics for dealing with opposition; and, sixth, an analysis of the other issues that the Moral Majority was collaterally pursuing.

"OUR CITIZENSHIP IS IN HEAVEN"

One of the very real barriers to the mobilization of the Moral Majority was the fundamentalist doctrine of separation. The doctrine preached the need for godly people to separate themselves strictly from doomed society and seek personal salvation through redemption. It was rooted in Biblical passages such as Philippians 3:20 and Ephesians 5:11. The fundamentalists translated Paul as saying, "For our citizenship is in Heaven." Ephesians 5:11 read, "have no fellowship with the unfruitful works of darkness, but rather reprove them."[2] For good or ill, fundamentalist preachers read in this, and other passages, an injunction to avoid becoming entangled in worldly politics.[3] The one true course was to associate only with other members of the regenerate body of Christ to study and worship. This personalistic bias in fundamentalist Christianity was often offered as an explanation for the near-absence of fundamentalists in politics during the past half-century.[4] One measure of this separation was the fact that, as of 1980, over 15 million fundamentalist adults had never voted, even though their pastors encouraged voting as one of the legitimate ways of "rendering unto Caesar the things which are Caesar's."[5] The Reverend Falwell offered a clear expression of this view in his 1965 sermon titled "Preachers and Politics," which had, particularly, preached on these texts and concluded "we have very few ties on this earth."[6] This sermon argued that ministers involved in the civil rights marches had strayed from their obligations and should return, posthaste, to their pulpits. The sermon concluded:

Love cannot be legislated. Love is found in a person—His Name is Jesus Christ. The church needs to become dedicated once again to the task of preaching Christ. Education, medicine, social reform, and all the other external ministries cannot meet the needs of the human soul and spirit . . . [but] when the light of the gospel shines into the sinner's heart, his entire life and attitudes are transformed. I feel that we need to get off the streets and back into the pulpits; we need to rededicate ourselves to the great task of turning this world back to God. The preaching of the gospel is the only means by which this can be done.

This doctrine created two difficulties for the Moral Majority's rhetors. First, they likely suffered a degree of cognitive dissonance as their involvement in politics led down a path contrary to deeply held religious convictions. Falwell himself noted this problem in his 1987 autobiography:

Since becoming a Christian I had lived a rather separatist life. I believed that "being yoked with unbelievers" for any cause was off limits. I didn't even get along very well with other kinds of Baptists, let alone with Methodists, Presbyterians, or Catholics . . . therefore, when I began considering how to put together a political organization that included all Americans I was faced with a terrific problem: my own personal psychological barrier. All of my background from Baptist Bible College and other places and persons providing my religious training made it difficult for me to consider such a prospect.[7]

This notion of separation is not unique to the fundamentalists. To a greater or lesser extent, all traditional religions preach a version of this doctrine. The Puritans, for example, were driven by their separatism to found their colonies in the New World, and, too, not all fundamentalists have adhered to the notion with equal fervor. Almost all fundamentalist sects have acceded to engage in politics when secular corruption proved so great that it threatened the ability of the church to survive in America.[8] Both the abolition and prohibition movements reflected such fundamentalist participation.

Nonetheless, Falwell's flock were susceptible to the separatist message. Separation was preached most consistently by southern fundamentalist preachers and was reinforced by a host of other factors. Southern fundamentalists were economically deprived and socially isolated, which made "the world's" appeal distant. They were, from the time of H.L. Mencken on, made the object of scornful derision by northerners and sophisticates everywhere.[9] Logically, then, Falwell's appeals had to create and continually renew the justification for breaching the wall of separation between the Saved and the secular world.

THE "I LOVE AMERICA" RALLIES

The "I Love America" rallies were held on the steps of forty-four state capitols during 1979 through 1981. The initial purpose of the rallies, which were hosted by the "Old-Time Gospel Hour," was to increase legislative support for the Christian school movement. To further this end, Falwell sought to bring together state legislators and members of the Christian school movement. He succeeded in gathering the right people at the rallies: the audiences numbered between 2,200 and 20,000, and almost all were the administrators, staff, faculty, and students of fundamentalist primary and secondary schools. The front row of seats was always reserved for the pastors who attended, and the rallies drew contingents from as many as seventy schools. Similarly, Falwell was able to attract some state legislators to each rally and the state's governor to over half of the rallies. Unfortunately, it appears that the rallies were a complete failure in their attempts to influence the course of legislation.[10]

In many ways, the 1979-81 rallies were a reprise of the Bicentennial rallies, which Falwell hosted in 1975 and 1976. In both cases, the rallies addressed large fundamentalist audiences with a combination of music, songs, and oratory. Weeks in advance of each rally, representatives of the "Old-Time Gospel Hour" alerted Christian schools in the region of the upcoming rally and offered to help provide the logistical support necessary to transport large numbers of people to the rally site. In the weeks before the rally, quarter- to full-page advertisements appeared in local newspapers; the ads typically featured a large photograph of the Reverend Falwell and an invitation to attend a rally in support of America. In the days immediately preceding the rally, two busloads of Falwell's college students were dispatched, and they were scheduled to arrive the night before the rally. The students began assembling equipment at 6:00 A.M., and by 9:30 A.M. would have set the stage, rehearsed, dressed, and prayed. By 12:30, the rally was over. Male students were assigned to disassemble the stage, while female students served as hostesses at a postrally luncheon sponsored by the Moral Majority. The entire event was over by 3:30 P.M., and the students embarked on an all-night bus trip to the next site.[11]

On a somewhat more relaxed schedule, Falwell, his body-guards, and other members of his personal entourage arrived in the church's private jet just before the rally began, addressed the rally, had lunch, and left. At the rallies, Falwell delivered five or six short speeches with music between each address. At the Columbia, South Carolina, rally, Falwell started by welcoming the crowd and spoke on America's moral decline. Music followed. The second speech praised our armed forces. The third tied America's military decline to a lack of leadership. A fourth reported that 84 percent of Americans surveyed by Gallup still believe in the Ten Commandments. Falwell alleged that the nation was being run by the other 16 percent, and went on to rally against abortion, pornography, homosexuality, and "all the God-haters in America . . . and the Liberals." During this same segment, Falwell called on the pastors to join the battle against these evils. "We better learn how to pull this country out of the gutter," he reminded them. "We better forget our little differences while we save our country." After a bit more music, Falwell returned to pound away at the litany of America's sins for another fifteen minutes before addressing his plan of action. He claimed that four steps were necessary: first, "we need a revival of prayer in our churches. . . . secondly, we need to be very informed . . . beyond that, we need to get our people registered to vote. . . . and then finally, we need to get involved." In his section on involvement, Falwell spoke of the beginning of a change that he saw and of a need to return to our covenant with the Lord. After the last segment of music, Falwell concluded with some kind words for the crowd, an invitation to a free lunch for the pastors and politicians, and a cheery story about the governor of Alabama's fervent support.[12] The rally ended without the Moral Majority being mentioned or even alluded to.

Following each rally, Falwell hosted a luncheon at a local hotel. No written records of these luncheons were kept, but we know that Falwell used them either to recruit leadership for a new state Moral Majority chapter or to strengthen support for the existing chapter. After each luncheon but before jetting off, Falwell held a news conference to announce either the creation of the state Moral Majority chapter or the installation of new supporters from among those attending the luncheon.

Although the rallies themselves were not sponsored by the Moral Majority, the appeals Falwell used in them were essentially the same as the appeals appearing in the first year of the *Moral Majority Report:* America is going to hell, immorality is the cause, Christian action is the solution. Also, as in the rallies, Falwell spent much of his time legitimating political action by arguing both that political action was consistent with his audiences' beliefs and that such action was the only guarantor of the survival of both Church and State.[13]

THE RHETORIC OF MOBILIZATION

Nineteen-eighty was the first year in which the *Moral Majority Report* was published and the first full year of the organization's existence. It was also the year in which the Moral Majority began serious attempts to create and sustain involvement in politics; the rallies of 1979 were one-shot affairs that helped to establish the structures of the Moral Majority, but did not provide the detailed and ongoing education necessary to sustain grassroots involvement. As a result, the *Moral Majority Report* devoted as much space to articles encouraging mobilization as it did to the ten next-most-important issues combined.

The Moral Majority's initial audience was the members of Falwell's church, the viewers the "Old-Time Gospel Hour," and the people contacted during the "I Love America" rallies.

Falwell faced three serious problems in attempting to energize this crowd: ignorance, apathy, and antipathy. First, these people were ignorant both about the Moral Majority and about how one gained political influence. Ignorance about the Moral Majority was predictable because the organization was young, although the Dallas-Fort Worth study reviewed in Chapter 2 also showed that the ignorance was enduring. The political ignorance was tied to the second problem, political apathy. Fundamentalists were, as noted earlier, encouraged to distance themselves from the secular world and from politics. The final problem was antipathy: the fundamentalists did not like politicians, and by and large, the politicians did not like the fundamentalists. We will examine this difficulty a bit more closely in this chapter's section on media coverage and criticism.

Mobilization stories advanced three main arguments in the face of these constraints; they claimed that Christian political action was (1) effective, (2) legitimate, and (3) necessary. We can refer to these as "can do," "may do," and "must do" claims. Stories in the first category centered on the various proofs that political action would be efficacious and on how to engage in effective political activity. A story on the Moral Majority's national convention, for instance, described the growing strength of the Christian political movement and the activities of the 2,000 convention attendees. At the convention, the pastors and laymen in attendance were told how to organize their state and local chapters, how to recruit workers, and how to become influential in politics.[14] The next issue of the *Report* featured a long story on the success of the Alaska Moral Majority in organizing and seizing control of the state's Republican Party. At the conclusion of another story in the same issue, one on Senator Paul Laxalt's "Family Protection Act" bill, there was a half-page story entitled, "What Citizens Can Do." The specific suggestions that made up this story illustrate the Moral Majority's "can do" themes:

1 . Write your two U.S. Senators and ask them to become co-sponsors of S. 1808, as amended. It is important to call it *S. 1808, as amended*. . . .

2. Write your Congressman and ask him to become a co-sponsor of *H.R. 6028, as amended*. . . .

3. Ask your friends to write letters. . . .

4. Address your letters as follows. . . .

5. Please do not use a form letter or copy someone else's letter. Originality is more important by far than grammatical perfection. Be polite, but be sure to ask him specifically to cosponsor the bill and ask him to respond to your letter.

6. Please send copies of your letter from *both* Senators and the Congressman to me at. . . .

7. *Do not write* to the following members of Congress who are already sponsors. . . .

    It is important that all of us write our Senators and Congressman. We should generate a million letters. Let's go. Now is the time.[15]

While this article was addressed to the general reader, the *Report* also wrote detailed articles for pastors and other opinion leaders. One article, "What Preachers Can Do Under the Law," stretched for two full pages and contained a detailed analysis of the tax code provisions that determined tax-exempt status. The second page of the article presented a detailed set of questions and answers that clarified the limits of permissible action by clergy:

Can a clergyman or officer of a nonprofit tax-exempt organization publicly endorse a candidate for political office . . .

Can it be done from the premises or pulpit of the tax-exempt organization . . .

Can the "organization" endorse a candidate . . .

Can the clergyman or nonprofit organization leader/officer lend his name to political advertisements and have his title listed . . .

Can a [tax-exempt] organization encourage or conduct voter registration or voter education activities among church members . . . on the non-profit premises. Must voter registration be non-partisan . . .

Can the organization spend money for paying registration organizers. . .

Can candidates speak on the premises . . .

Can public incumbent office holders speak on the premises or from the pulpit . . .

Can [a tax-exempt] organization . . . operate forums where all candidates for a particular office come and speak . . .

Can funds be raised at religion services for campaign contributions . . .[16]

Each of these questions received, first, a "yes" or "no" answer and, then, a detailed analysis about specific conditions that must be met in order to qualify for that answer.

Supplementing these specific action guides were more general stories that also supported the claim that "we can do it." These stories included encomia to President-elect Reagan, and frequent reports of local- and state-level success. Also notable was the Moral Majority's penchant for printing testimonials from those outside of the movement. Hence, there was front-page coverage of stories about support from Catholic, Protestant, and Jewish religious leaders, as well as from elected officials.[17] These stories seemed to serve several functions: first, they let the faithful know that there were like-minded allies available for the coming battle. Second, they legitimized the actions of the faithful by showing that respected people condoned those actions. Third, and perhaps most important, they legitimized the involvement of sympathetic outsiders who might have been deterred from participating by the notion that the Moral Majority was a narrowly fundamentalist organization. By demonstrating its breadth of support, however, the organization declared that those outside of the fundamentalist camp had a rightful place in the Moral Majority.

The second theme under "Mobilization" is "you may do it." These stories argued that the participation of clerics and religious citizens was both right and natural. These stories were of special importance given the rhetorical constraints mentioned above.

A variety of articles can be used to illustrate the Moral Majority's arguments that Christians can legitimately become involved in politics. For example, the executive director of the Moral Majority wrote an article entitled, "Out of the Pews, Into the Precincts," in which he sought to answer:

The honest objections of Christian involvement in government [which] can be traced to five basic questions:

*Jesus never said anything about politics, so why should we Christians become involved?

*Aren't we tearing down the wall of separation between Church and State?

*Do politics and religion mix?

*Because politics is dirty, won't a Christian have to compromise to participate?
*Won't active participation in politics weaken the work of the church, especially the effectiveness of preachers?[18]

Billings, the director, answered each of these questions in detail, and concluded that "God is looking for those who hold both pew and precinct in proper perspective, who will actively participate in keeping both church and country free."

Two months later, the Moral Majority offered a full-page, unsigned article that addressed many of these same questions. After retelling the story of David and Goliath, and after explaining which role the Moral Majority was taking, the author wrote that "listed below are a few of the types of opposition you will face as you get involved for God in the political arena. Following each 'argument' is God's answer from the Bible." The questions-cum-arguments were:

1. "Separation of Church and State Prohibits My Involvement as a Christian and Preacher Trying to Influence Public Policy". . . .

2. "Politics Are Dirty; Therefore Christians Shouldn't be Involved in 'Politics'". . . .

3. "The Old Testament Promises, Which Refer to Israel, Cannot be Applied to America". . . .

4. "Jesus and the apostles never tried to change the Roman government". . . .

5. "According to Bible Prophecy, We Know That Things Are Going to Get Worse, So Why Try?"[19]

Both of these examples represented works written by the Moral Majority and both explicitly used God to undergird their logic. Other stories, however, made the same point through secular sources. In one story, the executive director of the Republican Study Committee covered the same ground, but drew his answers from political analogies and his own experience, rather than from scriptural references.[20]

The third claim made in the "Mobilization" articles is "you must do it." These articles stressed the fact that Christians had a unique contribution to make: a contribution that secular political activists, no matter how well-intentioned, could not replace.

The claim was advanced in a somewhat less visible manner. Whereas the first two claims were advanced in large, headlined articles, "must do" claims were suffused throughout stories without ever rising to headline prominence.

Because these claims were not developed at great length, we can offer only short examples of them. An article on the Moral Majority convention, for example, contained Falwell's claim that "if America is ever to be turned from its course leading to destruction, then it is the pastors of America [who] must lead the way." In an article on voter registration drives, Robert Billings asserted that, "it is absolutely imperative that every Christian register and vote this year!" Similarly, in defining "the Awakening Giant," *Moral Majority Report* editor Harry Covert spoke of "that segment of moral and Christian America which is now becoming more aware of its responsibilities to God and country." Finally, a two-page article on a televised debate between Falwell and former representative Father Robert Drinan ran under the headline: "Nation's Moral Tailspin Reflects Church Apathy."[21] As these examples indicate, the uniqueness of the Christian perspective was more often assumed than argued.

To recapitulate, the most frequent theme of 1980 was the need for Christian mobilization, and this claim was supported by three types of warrants. The first argued that political activity was effective in producing the desired moral changes, and we have labeled this the "can do" issue. The second set of arguments addressed the reticence of conservative Christians to become involved in politics and attempted to pre-empt the challenges that they would predictably encounter; this was the "may do" issue. Our final set of arguments infiltrated many articles without being the sole focus of any of them; this was the "must do" issue, and it claimed that the reader had not only a right to act, but also a solemn responsibility to do so.

A WEALTH OF ATTENTION, A HOST OF CRITICS

The Moral Majority's notoriety, if not popularity, skyrocketed after the November 1980 elections. That election saw the installation of a conservative president and the ouster of a number of highly visible, liberal representatives and senators. Representatives of both the secular and Christian New Right immediately began claiming credit for the election outcomes. Some defeated liberal incumbents and challengers furthered this perception by shifting responsibility for their defeats from themselves to the machinations of the New Right. Jim Folsom, an Alabama Democrat who had upset the incumbent senator during the primary but who lost during the general election, claimed, for example, that the Moral Majority "had a tremendous effect on my defeat." With time, it became convenient for many defeated liberals and their campaign organizers to point to the devil of the New Right as the explanation for their losses, largely because this proved to be such an effective fund-raising strategy. Subsequent analyses suggested that the Religious Right's influence on the election was nearly negligible, but these findings were too late and too inconvenient to alter materially the perception that 1980 was The Year of the Religious Right.[22] The election, and a subsequent counter-organizing move by liberals, set the stage for the issues of 1981.

This year was dominated by reported attacks on the Moral Majority and the organization's attempted replies. Three of the top five issues addressed in the *Moral Majority Report* were aimed, directly or indirectly, at the Moral Majority's opponents; these issues were: attacks on the organization, failings of the liberal media, and a proposed boycott of television advertisers. In order to understand the issues raised, this section will review the nature of the charges leveled against the Moral Majority, a subject also covered in Chapter 1, and the following section will address the Moral Majority's response.

Briefly, 1981 was a high point in the controversy surrounding the Moral Majority: it was the subject of over one hundred general-interest magazine articles, seventy "national newspaper" articles, and involved in thirty network evening newscasts as either the subject of the report or as a source in it.[23] Also, if the pattern set by CBS News is typical, it was involved in sixty to seventy other network telecasts.[24] The arguments raised against the Moral Majority were placed into six general categories by Dinesh D'Souza in his authorized biography of Falwell:

The media barrage against Falwell is expressed in six ways: (1) Falwell is an absolutist, (2) Falwell wants to impose his views on everyone else, (3) Falwell is like the Ayatollah Khomeini, Adolph Hitler and Jim Jones rolled into one, (4) Falwell is racist, sexist and anti-Semitic, (5) Falwell is rolling in money, (6) Falwell and his supporters are stupid, weird, and "ultraconservative."[25]

Another way of illustrating the responses to the Moral Majority is to look at the way that the evening news programs covered the Moral Majority in 1981.[26] In January, ABC featured a forty second story on abortion, in which Falwell was quoted concerning the *Roe* decision. That same month, NBC reported that an interview with Falwell was to appear in *Penthouse* magazine, and ABC reported that Falwell had filed suit against *Penthouse* to halt distribution of the issue.

There was no network coverage in February, although that was the month that Falwell helped form the controversial Coalition for Better Television. Moral Majority reported that correspondents from all three networks were present at the news conference announcing the founding.[27]

In March, a CBS story announced that the Moral Majority was leading the drive to censor books, films, and record albums. The correspondent involved neither offered specific examples to substantiate this claim nor quoted any national Moral Majority leader. Instead, substantiation was limited to the assertion that "the group called Moral Majority has taken the lead in such efforts" and to a quotation from a Washington state Moral Majority leader complaining that children learn sex education more thoroughly than they do reading.[28]

In April, coverage included discussing the possibility that the Moral Majority would oppose the re-election of Massachusetts Senator Edward Kennedy. Again, the Moral Majority was not quoted but was referred to by the correspondent. NBC, in a story on child abuse, noted that there were efforts in some states to repeal child-abuse laws, and that the Moral Majority was involved in the repeal attempt. Without an exact transcript, it is difficult to assess this claim. The national organization had not publicly opposed child-abuse laws per se and had, indeed, called for stricter enforcement of laws on the books. It did, however, oppose a domestic violence bill that contained a provision related to child abuse; the primary objection was that the legislation called for an excessive degree of federal involve-ment.[29] It is possible that some of the local chapters were opposing child-abuse laws for some reason, but neither the *Moral Majority Report* nor the newspaper indices provided specific details by which this claim could be corroborated. The final story was a thirty second ABC report noting that Falwell and Coalition for Better Television President Donald Wildmon had challenged the presidents of the three television networks to a debate over programming. They were turned down.

There was no coverage in May. In June, the media addressed the Moral Majority's role in two substantive issues. On the fourth of June, both CBS and NBC noted that the Moral Majority supported legislation allowing tuition tax credits for the parents of students enrolled in private schools. NBC provided footage of Falwell, while CBS merely noted Falwell's support. The Moral Majority was not "pushing" these tax credits during 1981, in the sense that there was no mention of them in the *Report* in the three months surrounding the telecasts, but they were elements of the overall agenda.

Later in June, two of the networks featured stories on the proposed boycott of those companies that advertised on "smutty" television programs. CBS and NBC both ran stories on June 17 announcing the boycott and reporting on the react-ions of the three networks' presidents. Each story quoted Wild-mon and the presidents, but not the Moral Majority representa-tives. The same two networks ran stories on June 29 on the canceling of the boycott. The Coalition for Better Television canceled the boycotts after several major advertisers, including Procter & Gamble, Miles Laboratories, Warner-Lambert, and SmithKline, withdrew their sponsorship of the contested programs. In both of these stories, Falwell appeared on the air.

The Moral Majority appeared incidentally in two other news-casts during the month. One of these concerned the rise of Senator Helms, and the other was a discussion of the links be-tween the New Right and the Republican Party.

The most controversial coverage of the year began in July with the nomination of Sandra Day O'Connor to the Supreme Court. The three networks ran six stories between July 7-14, and the stories focused on Falwell's opposition to O'Connor's nomination. On July 7, ABC claimed that Falwell and conservative fund-raiser Richard Viguerie pledged to campaign against O'Connor. That same day, CBS reported that the Moral Majority opposed the nomination. The next day, ABC reported two related stories: President Reagan's discussions with Senator Helms and Falwell, and Senator Goldwater's infamous condemnation of Falwell. NBC ran a similar story. The next day, CBS ran a story on the right-wing opposition to the nomination and, again, quoted Goldwater on Falwell. The final story in the series was ABC's coverage on July 14, which reported that Falwell might support O'Connor, if Senator Helms did so. The remarkable things about these stories were that Falwell never appeared on camera and was never directly quoted. In order to prove Falwell's opposition to O'Connor, the correspondents either asserted his opposition or quoted Goldwater, who asserted Falwell's opposition.

This story highlighted one of the difficulties of our undertaking. Did Falwell oppose the O'Connor nomination? The Moral Majority never publicly disseminated information to that effect. The *Moral Majority Report* coverage stressed a cautious reservation unless and until O'Connor clarified her position on abortion. Additionally, none of Falwell's mass-mailed letters concerned the O'Connor nomination.[30] There were no quotations by Moral Majority representatives, either on the network news or in any of the newspapers covered by the National Newspaper Index. This does not, however, rule out the possibility that Falwell blurted out some negative comment in one of his twenty weekly speaking engagements or that he made a comment that could be construed to prove his opposition. Falwell and the Moral Majority strenuously denied ever having opposed the O'Connor nomination, although once Falwell's official position became one of support for the nominee, it became unlikely that the Moral Majority would ever admit to having opposed her. Because of this incomplete public record, it is unlikely that we will ever be able to make an unequivocal judgment concerning the initial coverage, although we can note that none of the networks chose to report on the position that Falwell publicly maintained, that is, that he withheld judgment until the facts were in.

Coverage of the Moral Majority in August was purely incidental. Falwell's name was mentioned in passing in one story.

In September, there were two minor and one major stories involving Falwell. The first minor story reported Falwell's attendance at an antiabortion convention in Dallas. The second minor story noted that Falwell met with Prime Minister Menachem Begin of Israel in the course of a debate over arms sales in the Middle East. The major story was Senator Goldwater's broadside against the New Right, which he denounced as divisive, and against Falwell, whom "every good Christian should kick in the ass." CBS and NBC both carried two minute and ten second stories involving the senator's comments, although neither quoted Falwell's replies nor those of other New Right activists.

In October, Falwell was briefly involved in a story concerning the closing of a Nebraska church school by state officials. While CBS spent nearly three minutes on the story, neither of its competitors covered it. There was no coverage in either November or December, except for one brief mention of Falwell attending a testimonial for presidential advisor Richard Allen.

To summarize: Falwell appeared with reasonable frequency on the national news, although it was rare that there was actual footage involved; more commonly, the position of the Moral Majority on a given issue was asserted. A number of these assertions were of questionable accuracy, as in the case of the child-abuse laws and the O'Connor nomination, although we cannot state with certainty that the networks were in error. It was rare that the network coverage reported items in Falwell's agenda, with the exceptions being tuition tax credits, the television boycott, and abortion. However, it was more common for Falwell's positions on miscellaneous items to be reported; such stories included: Helm's rise to power, the coverage of the Republian Party's rise, and Kennedy's reelection campaign. It does not appear that Falwell was the object of a "smear campaign," but it is likely that the news demonstrated a negative bias towards his organization. This bias may be inferred from the fact that the organization was not permitted to speak for itself, but rather, had its positions asserted and that the organization was not permitted the right to respond to attacks on it, such as Goldwater's.

THE RHETORIC OF REFUTATION AND SELF-PITY

Predictably, Falwell took all of this attention rather poorly. Writers in the *Report* claimed that "there are constant stories" misrepresenting the Moral Majority's agenda and that "every day, news articles, photography, TV newscasts or newspaper editorials are distorted." Moral Majority board member Timothy LaHaye implied the presence of a vast conspiracy operating to destroy the Moral Majority when he observed that all of the negative coverage had begun at once, as if some great central switch had been thrown. Falwell himself claimed that over forty-eight anti-Moral Majority groups were established in a single month.[31]

Falwell classified the purveyors of these attacks into four main groups. The largest group was the "liberal critics," those gadflies outside of both government and media who spent their time degrading the organization. The most frequently named group was Lear's People for the American Way, and the second most frequent were unnamed "critics," with Bartlett Giamatti, Rabbi Alexander Schindler, actor Tony Randall, and the American Civil Liberties Union also falling into this category. The second largest group was the "liberal media," which was most often addressed only by that general term. There were comparatively rare mentions of individual or specific organizations; these included: *Newsweek*, the *Los Angeles Times*, and the presidents of the television networks. The third largest group was the "liberal politicians." Like the media, these were most often addressed corporately rather than specifically, although Senators Goldwater and Kennedy, Governor Milliken of Michigan, and former senator McGovern were all mentioned by name. The final category was "the pornographers," who were rarely named and who included television programmers.

We should note that this is a rhetorically very restricted list. Not only were there no "real Americans" cited among those with reservations about the Moral Majority, but there was also

no category under which they might be included. Falwell did
not appear to recognize the possibility that people of good will
might be opposed to his initiatives on purely substantive
grounds. Despite his frequent protestations, this particular
sample suggests that his opponents did, indeed, constitute an
"immoral minority."

Just as the Moral Majority tended to address their opponents
generically, rather than individually, they took a similar
approach to evaluating the criticisms raised against them.
Indeed, Falwell claimed that "few, if any, of the critics of the
Moral Majority ever want to deal substantively with the
issues."[32] Perhaps as a result, Falwell rarely dealt substantively
with their criticisms. Instead, he derided his critics as
"individuals who are determined to push for their own
causes," as people who were "totally biased," and whose
coverage's "only consistent chord . . . had been distortion."[33]

There were several instances in which Falwell did choose to
report and respond to substantive criticisms. The first story
concerned the Moral Majority's response to an American Civil
Liberties Union (ACLU) advertisement that pictured a grim
Moral Majoritarian brandishing an outsized cross (labeled
"Moral Majority" for those who did not take the hint from the
headline: "If the Moral Majority Has Its Way, You'd Better Start
Praying") and riding on the back of a saddled-and-bridled Uncle
Sam. Surrounding the illustration were a number of paragraphs
of text in which the ACLU made many accusations. The *Report*
provided a full-page reprint of the ACLU ad, with the individual
paragraphs numbered and numbered responses on the next
page. For example, paragraph number three read: "if they
believe that birth control is a sin, then you should not be
allowed to use contraceptives." The corresponding response
was "3) Moral Majority has never taken a position on birth
control."[34]

Since the entire ACLU ad was reproduced, there was no question as to whether the Moral Majority fairly presented the criticism. Unfortunately, both sides advanced arguments that were
either erroneous or deceptive. For example, the ACLU charged
that "the Moral Majority raises a million dollars a week with its

television program." This claim was flawed by two errors: first, the Moral Majority's budget for 1980 was about $2 million, and second, it did not have a television program. The source of this error was in attributing aspects of the "Old-Time Gospel Hour" to the Moral Majority. In another instance, the ACLU claimed that "a week after the election, [Falwell] warned elected officials, both Republican and Democrat, to 'get in step' or 'prepare to be unemployed.'" While Falwell doubtless endorsed the statement, he did not make it; the speaker was Paul Weyrich of the Committee for the Survival of a Free Congress.

Then again, the quality of the Moral Majority's argument was not substantially higher. When, for example, ACLU charged that "if they believe that a man should be the breadwinner and the divinely appointed head of the family, then the law should keep women in their place," we had a charge that was factually untrue but that was designed to support a larger claim. That is, the ACLU seemed to be making the point of the Moral Majority's intolerance and coerciveness rather than just its position on women's rights; this interpretation is supported by the fact that most of the first column of the ad was devoted to documenting the group's coerciveness through a series of "if . . . then" propositions: "if they believe X, then they will force you to submit to X." The Moral Majority's response was "that this is grade A baloney and the ACLU knows it. We support full equal rights for women, though we believe the E.R.A. is the wrong way to bring it about." This addressed the ACLU's generalization with a directly contrary Moral Majority assertion, but it did not address the underlying claim supported by this entire series of examples. The Moral Majority also failed to address several portions of the advertisement, as when the ACLU alleged that the Moral Majority supported legislation that would strip federal courts of their right to hear certain types of cases nor did they address the ACLU's defense of the Moral Majority's right to exist and pursue their opinions. At the very least, these omissions direct the reader's attention away from those aspects of the advertisement, and at worst, they constitute tacit acquiescence to the charge. The Moral Majority's strategy appeared to be to highlight the most outrageous errors and egregious statements made by their opponents and to emphasize factual errors. More restrained objections were either not answered or were answered with nonresponsive invective (e.g., "baloney").

The Moral Majority made the same sort of explicit recognition and response on two other occasions: in September with Giamatti's statements, and in both September and October with Goldwater's.[35] In each case, the strategy was the same. Both speeches were represented by no more than a sentence or two extracted from the speech; then again, both speeches were sufficiently polemical that a fair sense of their content could be gained by a reasonably short excerpt. Both speakers were subjected to extended ad hominem attack, although there is an argument that their own addresses made sufficient use of this tactic to legitimate similar replies. For Giamatti, we were told that "to be lectured on the perils of the Moral Majority upon entering Yale is on the order to being lectured on the danger of bedbugs on entering a brothel."[36] Another commentator noted that Giamatti was "a man of reported political ambitions who has chosen to pander for popularity among media elites, at the expense of the truth."[37] Similarly, Goldwater was dismissed as having delivered "mindless, lopsided blasts." "Conservatism's oldest living totem," we were told, had been passed by time, and his charges were condescendingly dismissed as the maunderings of an old man whose mind had been unhinged by the pain of an unsuccessful hip operation.[38] The greater part of the coverage of each speech was consumed by Moral Majority statements that contradicted those of its opponents. Hence, the Moral Majority took issue with five of Giamatti's substantive claims and six of Goldwater's.

Falwell's strategies for dealing with criticism, then, were comparatively simple. In large part, they consisted of labeling, impugning, and ignoring those who publicly objected to the Moral Majority. They were lumped together as unnamed "critics" or untrusted "liberal media." They were alleged to be using distortion against the organization as part of a conspiratorial effort to maintain the secular humanists' control. For the most part, their charges were either ignored or misrepresented to be more easily refuted.

These strategies allow us to make some inferences about the

audience the Moral Majority presumed it was addressing. Chiefly, we can see that the audience was assumed to be the same unquestioning flock inherited from the "Old-Time Gospel Hour." The strategies used in refutation were efforts to dismiss, rather than refute, the opposition. In order to have any confidence in this strategy, the Moral Majority had to assume that the audience was willing to do the same. If a diverse audience were assumed, contrarily, the organization would have needed to persuade the readers of the rightness of its positions, but it did not. This inference is consistent not only with the mobilization and legitimation appeals discussed earlier, which explicitly focused on the responsibilities of Christian citizens, but also with the Moral Majority's approach to the remainder of its agenda in this period.

RANDOM RHETORIC

While we should be reticent to apply the term "random" to the agenda of a large and influential organization, such as the Moral Majority, it nevertheless seems to be an apt description of the 1980-81 agenda. The Report devoted entire articles to nearly seventy different subjects, which ranged from indicting the proposed nine-digit Zip Code to airing the complaints of a female soldier who felt "defeminized," from degeneracy in the Carter White House to the family rent tax, and from the evils of the Legal Aid Services Corporation, a government agency providing legal aid to the indigent, to waste in government. None of these issues ever resurfaced, and few appeared to have particular relevance to the Moral Majority's essential concerns. Still, in issue after issue, these one-of-a-kind stories appeared.

In Chapter 1, it was speculated that this might reflect a simple matter of convenience: the Reverend Falwell chose to buy or commission a variety of articles by outsiders, because it was easier than diverting resources from the task of mobilization. Too, this strategy may have furthered the legitimation of the organization by bringing work by a host of easily recognizable figures into the *Report*. The immediate relevance of this diversity was to lend some context to our discussion of the remaining major issues in the *Report* over these years. Because so many issues were covered, none were covered in great depth other than the legitimation and mobilization claims already discussed. This means that the second most frequent issue in each year was a distant second and the fifth most frequent issue garnered little more attention than the twentieth.

The other issues of 1980 can be summarized quite briefly, then. The second most common issue concerned election results; these appeared about one-third as frequently as mobilization articles and were, predictably, clustered in October through December. In substance, these articles generally focused on the election of pro-moral politicians in the November general election and discussed the types of changes that were possible, if not guaranteed, given a government that was increasingly sympathetic to the Moral Majority's perspective.

It is not until we come to the third position that we find a "substantive" issue: the return of voluntary prayer to the public schools. This was a year of considerable legislative activity on the school-prayer issue, with Senators Helms and Laxalt and Representative Crane all pushing separate bills that would further the school-prayer cause, so it was not surprising that this was the most common substantive issue. The next two issues, also substantive, occurred with nearly the same frequency as school prayer did. They were support for Israel and the various aspects of the gay-rights controversy. The pro-Israel prominence was probably engendered by two factors. First was Prime Minister Menachem Begin's decision to embrace warmly the Moral Majority's foreign policy, which made him the first head of state to recognize the organization. The second was the organization's desire to dispel the notion that it was anti-Semitic. The concern for Israel was evinced only in 1980; after that year, there was virtually no mention of that nation in the *Report*.

The most curious finding was not what was covered, but what was not covered. Specifically, the issue of abortion did not appear in the ten most commonly raised issues in 1980. Since no Moral Majority figure has ever addressed the question of how these priorities were determined, there was no official explanation for this state of affairs, and there was no outside article that addressed the issue. Several explanations are possible. One was that there was no legislative action on abortion in 1980, so there was nothing to report. This seems unlikely since many other issues not in the news were covered. A second guess is that the Moral Majority thought there were enough incidental mentions of abortion in other articles that a major article was not yet warranted. A third guess is that the Moral Majority had enough faith in its audience that it felt this issue did not need to be pushed; that is, most of the early members of the Moral Majority were either members of Falwell's church or viewers of the "Old-Time Gospel Hour" and both of these forums addressed the abortion issue. It may have been that the organization felt that it would be a better use of scarce resources to cover issues in the *Report* that could not be addressed by the church. This explanation suffered from the fact that it assumed some central coherence to the Moral Majority's agenda-setting; our survey suggests this coherence was absent. Finally, this situation might be purely coincidental. That is, abortion was not discussed because there was no central control of the agenda, which meant that the organization was not yet pursuing coverage of specific issues, and because no suitable outside article happened to crop up. This possibility seems entirely consistent with the scattered and somewhat haphazard nature of the organization early in its history.

This was a remarkable year for the Moral Majority agenda. The most important issue had a wider lead over the second most important issue than any issue in any year. Yet this issue of mobilization and legitimation disappeared with the start of 1981, and did not reappear again for four years. The second leading issue, election results, never again received substantial coverage in the *Report*. With the defeat of the various legislative initiatives concerning school prayer, it, too, dropped out of the leading issues, and did not reappear until 1983 and 1984. The coverage of Israel, effectively, ended with 1980, and the antihomosexual articles did not appear again for several years. Contrarily, the ignored issue of abortion dominated the organization's agenda over four of the next five years.

As with 1980, the remainder of 1981's agenda can be summarized rather briefly. Abortion became the second-leading issue in 1981, and its scope rivaled that given to dealing with anti-

Moral Majority attacks. Yet the coverage given to abortion was still somewhat peculiar. About half of all the space devoted to this issue was given over to covering research by the Upjohn Company; this research was supposed to be leading to the development of a home "abortion pill."[39] It appeared that Upjohn was producing a suppository and was working to produce a capsule that were capable of inducing menstruation, ipso facto triggering an abortion. The *Report* ran two, four-plus page articles, the longest in its history, in consecutive issues; these stories provided some background information, official company statements, and the Moral Majority's speculations concerning the product. While the Moral Majority's concern was entirely understandable since the availability of an at-home abortifacient would make legislative control of abortion virtually impossible, it was less understandable why this issue disappeared after the September 21, 1981, issue. If the Moral Majority's suspicions were well-founded, we should wonder why the deadly Upjohn discoveries were never again mentioned in the *Report*.

The remainder of abortion reporting was somewhat more conventional. The Moral Majority ran several articles that denounced the sin of abortion and two that provided background information on the controversy. Finally, they ran five stories supporting mobilization against abortion (i.e., they discussed the prospects for success of Senator Hatch's proposed Human Life Amendment, the general prospects of the pro-life movement, and how to become effectively involved in curbing abortion).

The third most common issue involved the evils of pornography. There were two worthwhile observations about this coverage. First, this was the most prominence ever given to pornography until the organization's last year. Second, the attacks on pornography often contained a tinge of hysteria comparable to that used in the abortion polemics. When speaking of pornography, Moral Majority made it clear that it was not just talking about hard-core depictions of horrible deviance. Rather, it found the themes in women's magazines, television programs, and contemporary music all pornographic. Its articles on televised pornography suggested a near-conspiratorial air when it alleged that "we are being programmed, subtly but steadily, to accept gross sin and immorality as normal." An accompanying article described risque television programming as "the worst disgrace and perhaps most dangerous influence on morality . . . since the introduction of drugs into our society." Later in that same issue, the Reverend LaHaye described the perfidious pedophilic crimes of "sex-crazed pornography readers," and a subsequent story linked the pornography industry to the spread of illegal drugs. Finally, an article on pornographers' attempts to discredit Falwell gratuitously contained a small picture of television producer Norman Lear.[40] During much of the year, the *Report* also ran a guest column on the family, which frequently highlighted the damaging effects of pornography. In one instance, a mother found smut under her child's bed, and in another, one found that her husband had been hiding pornographic pictures all around the house; not only was their marriage shaken, but the poor woman was also unable to continue her housework for fear of encountering depictions even more vulgar than those she had already ferreted out.[41]

The casting of this rather broad net is more explicable once we consider the next two issues on the Moral Majority's agenda: depradations by the liberal media and the proposed boycott of companies that bought advertising time on objectionable television programs. These are two closely related topics, with the former identifying the problem and the latter its solution. Thus, the Moral Majority ran one set of articles that examined television's failings in depth and another set that discussed the proposed boycott.

This becomes particularly coherent when we tie these three issues back to the leading issue: attacks on the Moral Majority. As noted, many of the attacks were initiated by the media, and all were transmitted by them. It seems reasonable to assume, since all of these issues were related, that the Moral Majority's agenda served as a self-reinforcing whole. The media were generally awful, which was proven both by their slander of the Moral Majority and their willingness to peddle pornography, which meant that they could not be trusted. This helped immunize the group's members from the force of the media's attacks. In addition, they certainly needed to be opposed through the boycott and by funding the Moral Majority. Thus, a number of issues that initially bore little relation to one another could be conceived as being intimately linked in their defense of the Moral Majority's legitimacy. If this claim is valid, it also suggests that the organization grew out of its early inability to focus its attention, and had the ability to shape and coordinate its agenda strategically. The extent of this issue control will be examined in Chapter 4.

In summary, the Moral Majority came into existence with a desire to change the world. Its ability to do this was predicated upon its ability to energize a mass of people to support its cause. The most obvious mass available to it, indeed the only group to whom it might plausibly appeal, was the supporters of the Reverend Falwell's various ministries. This group was characterized by deeply held convictions; this was good in the sense that the congruence of their convictions with the organization's freed the Moral Majority from the necessity to argue extensively for its agenda. The audience needed, at most, the occasional prods and horror stories that strengthened their resolve. These same convictions were bad because one of the convictions was antipolitical; that is, most of these Christians did not see political participation as being consistent with their desire for salvation.

The Moral Majority responded to this situation by devoting the greatest part of its suasory powers to convincing its members that the members' apolitical leanings were, at best, outmoded and, at worst, a betrayal of their obligations. The Moral Majority argued that there were tasks that its members could, might, and must do; these included voting and providing financial support to conservative causes. The Moral Majority also sought to engender something of a siege mentality by recounting the volumes of treacherous opposition to its attempts to return America to the path that God had set.

What the organization did not do was talk about its issues. Given the homogenous audience it addressed, such discussion was unnecessary. As the organization attempted to broaden its base of support to encompass a more religiously diverse, though politically compatible, audience, the organization needed to change its appeals. The shape of these changes is discussed in the following chapter.

NOTES

1. Jerry Falwell, "Capitol Report," August 1979, p. 1. The "Capitol Report" was a short-lived newsletter, printed on the front and back of one legal-sized page. The front page has a picture of Falwell in front of the Capitol building, and its sole article was untitled.

2. Harvey Cox, *Religion in the Secular City* (New York: Simon and Schuster, 1984).

3. It is important to remember, though, that separation was a selective phenomenon. It seemed more important in the political and social realms than in the economic one. Hence, fundamentalists might seek after the goods of a secular society and hold good-paying jobs, but still avoid becoming active in partisan politics or in nonchurch social organizations.

4. Robert Wuthnow, "The Political Rebirth of American Evangelicals," in *The New Christian Right*, Robert Liebman and Robert Wuthnow, eds. (Hawthorne, NY: Aldine Publishing 1983), pp. 165-185; "Insiders Look at Fundamentalism," *The Christian Century*, 18 November 1981, p. 1196; "Mainstream U.S. Evangelicals Surge in Political Influence," *New York Times*, 14 March 1982, pp. 1, 50.

5. Jerry Falwell, "An Interview with the Lone Ranger of American Fundamentalism," *Christianity Today* 4 September 1981, pp. 22-23.

6. Jerry Falwell, "Preachers and Politics," sermon delivered 21 March 1965, reprinted in Perry Young, *God's Bullies* (New York: Harper, Row & Winston, 1982), pp. 310-317.

7. Jerry Falwell, *Strength for the Journey* (New York: Pocket Books, 1987), pp. 343, 345.

8. Frances Fitzgerald, "A Disciplined, Charging Army," *The New Yorker*, 18 May 1981, pp. 127-128; "Lone Ranger" interview, pp. 23-24.

9. Fitzgerald, "Charging Army," pp. 111-112; David Harrell, "The Roots of the Moral Majority: Fundamentalism Revisited," *Occasional Papers* (Collegeville, MN: Institute for Ecumenical and Cultural Research, 1981), pp. 7-9; Sean Wilentz, "God and Man at Lynchburg," *The New Republic*, 25 April 1988, pp. 30-31.

10. Roy E. Buckelew, "The Political Preaching of Jerry Falwell: A Rhetorical Analysis of the Political Preaching of the Rev. Jerry Falwell in Behalf of the Moral Majority During the 1980 Political Campaign," diss., University of Southern California, 1983; telephone interview with Roy Buckelew, 6 September 1986. Mr. Buckelew's work represented the only coherent body of secondary material on the "I Love America" rallies. While there were passing references to the rallies in a number of secondary sources, none spent any time discussing the staging and significance of the rallies. Moreover, while there was local newspaper

coverage of each rally, the journalistic conventions on reporting dictated virtual exclusion of the rhetorical situation from the story in favor of reporting on the substance of the Reverend Falwell's remarks.

11. Randy Rebold, "Memorandum to Members of the LBC Faculty," typewritten. Mr. Rebold was Director of the "I Love America" rallies for the "Old-Time Gospel Hour," and he circulated a detailed discussion of the timing of the rallies and the responsibilities of Falwell's traveling students in order to convince Liberty Baptist faculty to allow the students to make up missed work.

12. Jerry Falwell, unpublished transcript of "I Love America" rally, Columbus, South Carolina, 31 March 1980. Mr. Buckelew kindly provided this transcript, which he commissioned from audio-tapes held by the Reverend Falwell's church. Several years after the rallies, a flood in Lynchburg destroyed the majority of the tape collection. Mr. Buckelew indicated that the Columbus rally was typical of all of the rallies for which records remain.

13. Ibid.

14. "700 Pastors, 1300 Church Workers Mobilized," *Moral Majority Report*, 14 March 1980, pp. 8-9. Hereafter cited as *Report*.

15. "Alaska's Political Structure 'Stirred Up,'" *Report* 11 April 1980, p. 16; "What Citizens Can Do," *Report*, 11 April 1980, p. 15. Underlined portions were bold-face in the original.

16. "What Preachers Can Do Under the Law," *Report*, 1 May 1980, pp. 15-16. In the original, all of these questions were presented in bold-face, and the answers were in light-face.

17. "Catholic 'Thrilled with Success' of Moral Majority," *Report*, 15 October 1980, p. 10; "Noted Presbyterian Leader Says Moral Majority Is 'Right,'" *Report*, 15 October 1980, p. 11; "Catholic, Jewish, Protestant Voters Main Contributor to Conservative Win," *Report*, 15 December 1980, p. 3; "Jewish Leaders Rebuke Schindler," *Report*, 15 December 1980, p. 11. Rabbi Alexander Schindler had publicly criticized the New Right.

18. Robert Billings, "Out of the Pew, Into the Precinct," *Report*, 14 March 1980, pp. 15-16.

19. "Six Questions Asked Most of Christians in Politics," *Report*, 1 May 1980, p. 10. The aberrant punctuation, capitalization, and numbering all occurred in the original.

20. "Dingman Says: Christians in Politics in No Way Violates Church-State Principle," *Report*, 6 June 1980, p. 4.

21. "Seven Hundred Pastors," p. 8; Robert Billings, "Sign Up Now," *Report*, 26 May 1980, p. 16; Harry Covert, "The Right of Responsibility Grows," *Report*, 15 September 1980, p. 2; Cal Thomas,

"Nation's Moral Tailspin Reflects Church Apathy," *Report*, 15 September 1980, pp. 4-5.

22. Seymour Lipset and Earl Raab, "The Evangelicals and the Election," *Commentary*, March 1981, pp. 25-32; "Right-Wing Coalition 'Has Little Effect on Election,'" *Report*, 13 March 1981, p. 7.

23. These counts are based on computerized searches of the *National Magazine Index*, which covers approximately 400 titles, and the *National Newspaper Index*, which covers the *New York Times, Washington Post, Christian Science Monitor, Wall Street Journal*, and several other "national" newspapers. The three network newscasts are covered in the *Television News Index and Abstracts* (Nashville: Vanderbilt University). Transcripts of all CBS programs are available through the *CBS News Index* (New York: Microfilming Corporation of America, 1981).

24. This figure was determined by comparing all mention of Falwell or the Moral Majority in the *CBS News Index* with the number of mentions associated specifically with the network's evening news program.

25. Dinesh D'Souza, *Falwell: Before the Millennium* (Lake Bluff, IL: Regnery-Gateway, 1984), p. 150.

26. Coverage again was determined by reference to the *Television News Index* and the *CBS News Index*.

27. Ron Godwin, "The Idea of Compelling Concessions: The Comparing of Berlin Book-burnings to the CBTV," *Report*, 20 April 1981, p. 3.

28. Eric Engberg, *CBS News Daily Broadcasts*, vol. seven, 11 March 1981.

29. "Surge of Child Abuse Cases Alarms Nation," *Report*, January 1985, p. 1; "Senate Jeopardizes Family Values," *Report*, 14 March 1980, p. 4.

30. Jerry Falwell, "Get the Facts Before Making Decision," *Report*, 20 July 1981, p. 3.

31. Jerry Falwell, quoted in D'Souza, *Falwell*, p. 34.

32. "Liberals Launch Vicious Attacks on 'New Right,'" *Report*, 16 March 1981, p. 12.

33. "Liberals Launch . . ."; "Noted California Author-Pastor Blasts Media for 'Misquoting, Twisting the Facts,'" *Report*, 20 April 1981, p. 7.

34. "ACLU Ad Filled with Libel," "Moral Majority Refutes ACLU Charges Point-by-Point," "ACLU Hysteria Insults Intelligence of Public," *Report*, 15 December 1980, pp. 8-9. The ACLU ad constituted the Moral Majority's first major response to public criticism.

35. William Rusher, "Goldwater and the Religious Right," *Report*, 19 October 1981, p. 7; "Goldwater: Time Has Passed Him," *Report*, 21

September 1981, p. 6; "Yale President Blasts Moral Majority," "Students Victims of Yale Tirade," *Report*, 21 September 1981, p. 7.

36. William F. Buckley, quoted in "Yale President . . . "

37. Howard Phillips, quoted in "Yale President . . . "

38. Rusher, "Goldwater," p. 7.

39. "Abortion to Be as Easy as Aspirin," *Report*, 24 August 1981, pp. 3-5; "Employees Uneasy About Abortion," *Report*, 21 September 1981, pp. 3-5, 8.

40. "Porno, Profanity Not Legal on TV," *Report*, 16 March 1981, p. 8; "Sex Business Is Good," *Report*, 16 March 1981, p. 9; "Porno Pushers Find Falwell Dangerous," *Report*, 16 March 1981, p. 17; "How Porn Industry Set Up the Dope Lobby," *Report*, 16 March 1981, p. 19; "Porn Kings to Discredit Moral Majority," *Report*, 16 March 1981, p. 19.

41. Glen Griffin, "Pornography Damages Marriages," *Report*, November 1981, p. 11; "Mom Finds Porn in Son's Room," *Report*, 20 July 1981, p. 14. All of Dr. Griffin's columns dealt with pornography, although it was not clear whether this meant that Griffin only wrote about pornography or the Moral Majority only bought those columns dealing with it.

Chapter Four

The Moral Majority Agenda: Change and Consistency

Moral Majority's position was clearly established in June of 1979 and it has not changed one iota since.
Jerry Falwell, 4 September 1981[1]

Compromise is a change of principle; strategy is a change of tactics. Never Change Principles!
Robert Billings, 14 March 1980[2]

By the beginning of 1982, the Moral Majority was ready to address the issues that gave it birth. Whereas its first two years were largely preoccupied with creating an effective political organization, the Moral Majority spent the next three years both educating the America public and becoming educated by it. By the end of this time, the organization had evolved a distinctly different agenda than it had at the outset.

When we consider the Moral Majority's agenda, we need to look both at what issues were stressed in a given year and at the ways in which the organization treated the issues it chose to address. Hence, it is not only relevant to consider whether the Moral Majority spent more time talking about abortion or pornography, but also whether the organization chose to say different things about abortion in 1982 than it did in 1985. In order to help keep these two questions distinct, we will divide this chapter into three sections. The first section will explain the coding system that allows us to determine the amount of emphasis given in the *Moral Majority Report* to any given issue. The second section will present a description of the organization's agenda for each of the four years in question and will serve as an overview of what the organization stressed. The third section will select several of the most important issues that have persisted across time and will look at changes in the ways that the organization addressed those issues.

THE CONTENT ANALYSIS SYSTEM

We can reconstruct the Moral Majority's agenda from different periods by using the *Moral Majority Report*, in which the organization presented its official, public claims. The frequent changes in the *Report*'s format and frequency of publication made it impossible to be highly precise in an assessment of the amount of space given to particular issues, but it will allow easy comparison of the relative weights given these issues.

This system for classifying articles consists of nine broad categories and more than 130 specific ones. The broad categories include the eight subject headings that defined the internal sections of *Moral Majority Report* in its last year, plus a ninth, labeled "Personalities in the News."[3] The 130 specific categories were arranged under the broad ones, and included, for example, abortion (under the broad heading of "Human Life"), gay rights (under "Morality"), and the nine-digit Zip Code (under "Politics and Government"). These narrow categories were constructed by listing all titles from a sample of every fourth issue of the *Report* and then grouping together specific stories into fairly concise categories. So, for example, one story on how one woman felt "defeminized" by being a soldier, another of a woman who objected to "barracks language," and a third on why women should not be admitted to the U.S. Military Academy at West Point were all joined under the heading, "Women in the Military," which came under the broad category of "National Security and Foreign Affairs."

Inevitably, some categories turned out to be much broader than others; for example, there was roughly equal coverage given to the White House Conference on the Family and to the notion of sexual degeneracy. Each category represented, however, a lowest common denominator. This means that there were no feasible subcategories into which these could be divided without giving each story its own heading. Finally, the broad category of "Politics and Government" was divided into three intermediary categories, called "Negative Government Actions," "Our Enemies," and "Contested Ground."[4] This was done both because the "Politics and Government" category was over twice the size of any other and because this breakdown helped to create a clearer idea of the issues being addressed. In the next section of this chapter, this system will be used to understand what issues were important in each of the years under examination.

RETURNING AMERICA TO MORAL SANITY: FUNDAMENTAL CONSISTENCY

While the Moral Majority's first three years showed a strong concern for organizational politics and the preservation of their movement, by 1982 the organization had gained a degree of legitimacy that allowed it to focus its energies on enacting a morally conservative agenda. This shift was, in part, demonstrable through changing media coverage of the Moral Majority. While the Moral Majority was the subject of sixty-eight "national newspaper" articles in 1981, it received less coverage than that, sixty-two articles, over the next four years combined. Similarly, it fell from coverage in one hundred magazine articles in 1981 to thirty-seven, fourteen, and six in the next three years. respectively.[5] The Majority seemed to sense this change and reflect it in its own coverage of the media. Calls for a television boycott ended in 1981; articles under "attacks on the Moral Majority" were more numerous in 1981 than in the next four years combined, as were articles attacking the liberal media. In short, it appears that the Moral Majority had won its right to be heard.

In comparison to our examination of the 1979-81 period, our look at 1982-85 is brief. The reason for this is that substantive issues had become predominant by this latter period. This allows us to be brief here, for two reasons. First, many of the issues are nearly self-explanatory. Second, these issues will reappear in the final section of this chapter, which concerns changes within issues across time. As a result, these next years will be presented somewhat synoptically.

1982

The agenda for 1982 showed a variety of old and new issues. While extensive coverage had previously been devoted to three of 1982's top five issues, two others received substantial attention for the first time, and even with the issues that had already been addressed, there were some shifts in emphasis.

Surprisingly, school prayer was the single largest issue for 1982, far outdistancing the second issue, abortion. This finding is surprising mainly because school prayer was not generally viewed as one of the core issues in the Moral Majority agenda.[6]

The dominance of school prayer was established by the *Report*'s May coverage of President Reagan's proposed school prayer amendment. Reagan generated considerable coverage for the issue with his decision to announce the amendment in a large Rose Garden ceremony that featured many conservative political and religious figures. The Moral Majority devoted a large amount of space in the May issue to supporting the amendment. While much of the space was devoted to the Rose Garden ceremony and to reprinting President Reagan's statement, an even larger amount was devoted to a defense of prayer in the schools. The three major articles and one full-page advertisement took up nearly one-third of the entire *Report*.[7]

The Moral Majority's defense of the amendment advanced two main claims: that school prayer was part of America's heritage and that such prayers were essential. The first claim was illustrated by Patrick Buchanan's citation of the Northwest Ordinance of 1787 and an 1811 New York Supreme Court case, and by Alfred Balitzer's extensive quotations from Presidents Washington and Jefferson and from Alexis deTocqueville.[8] The more immediate, prudential claims included Cal Thomas's statement that, ''since [the Supreme Court's ruling on school

prayer], the nation has seen a marked increase in school vanda-
lism, a decline in respect for authority, drug usage has become
an epidemic, and unwanted pregnancies and venereal disease
have been rampant.''[9] The Moral Majority attributed the failure
of the initiative to make any legislative headway by the end of
the year to a predictable trio of forces: President Reagan's failure
to make any real effort in support of the bill after the Rose
Garden ceremony, the willingness of a minority of congressmen
to continue thwarting the wishes of the Moral Majority, and the
Supreme Court's continued misreading of the Constitution.[10]

The second leading issue, abortion, received considerably nar-
rower coverage. While the school-prayer issue was the subject
of a major effort to educate the readers about its merits, the
abortion coverage focused heavily on reporting the rise and fall
of several legislative initiatives. The legislation in question was
the Human Life Amendment to the Constitution, proposed by
Senator Orrin Hatch of Utah, and an amendment to an amendment to a bill to raise the national debt ceiling. This latter
measure was proposed by Senator Jesse Helms of North Carolina. The advantage that Helms's bill held over Hatch's was that
Hatch's bill stood alone and required the vote of sixty senators,
while Helms's was attached to a bill that was almost certain to
pass and that required only a simple majority vote. The introduction of these bills was the subject of two *Report* cover stories,
including pictures of Senator Helms, Senator Hatch, and a fetus.

While the rise of the abortion bills received page-one coverage, their ultimate demise was buried on page six, and appeared
after stories on the closing of two church schools, the need for
belief in God, the school-prayer bill, and the failings of the too
moderate president of the Southern Baptist Convention. As with
the school-prayer bill, the Moral Majority rationalized the failure
of the abortion bills by attributing it to "parliamentary
maneuverings," rather than any intrinsic fault of its position.[11]

The third issue was not connected with the legislative process;
this was the closing of two church schools for operating without
state approval. In one, a pastor was arrested, and in the other,
the school was padlocked. The Moral Majority's coverage portrayed the strife as a major constitutional and moral question
that directly threatened the survival of the Christian school

movement. In one case, the school was described as having been "ransacked" by state officials, and the other was involved in a "fight for life against the state."[12] The issue was sufficiently important to evoke calls for civil disobedience from both a guest columnist and from Moral Majority Vice-Presient Ron Godwin. Edwin Rowe, the columnist, wrote that:

When confronted with a choice between the obedience to God and obedience to government, we must echo the words of Peter and the other apostles who steadfastly refused to curtail their service for Christ and cast into the teeth of the tyrants this immortal precept: "We ought to obey God rather than men" (Acts 5:29).[13]

Godwin, additionally, suggested that these attacks might be the trigger that finally "awakened the giant" and created "a movement of historic proportions." He speculated that:

It is curious that the flood tide of abortions sweeping the land has not fully awakened the conservative-religious giant, perhaps because abortions are private acts; but when assaults were made directly on churches and on Christian ministers in Nebraska, the alarm rang all over America. And we have not heard the last of this crisis.[14]

This was true: the Moral Majority began and ended 1983 with a spate of church school stories and made the attacks on church schools its dominant issue in 1984.

The coverage of the fourth leading story, the Equal Rights Amendment, returned to the pattern of linking coverage to actions that concerned legislation. In January, the Moral Majority reported that a federal judge in Idaho had ended the ERA with a two-pronged ruling: first, that Congress' decision to extend the time for ratification had been unconstitutional, and second, that states had the right to rescind their passage of the Amendment. They also reported in June that three more states had refused to ratify the Amendment, which effectively terminated it, even if the Idaho judge's ruling has been later overturned.[15] Like the abortion coverage and unlike school prayer, coverage of the ERA's demise was tightly focused on reporting, with little or no effort to debate the issue.

Finally, the Moral Majority continued its indictment of the liberal communications media. If this category is narrowly construed, then the allegations were that the media portrayed far too much sexual activity, that it was controlled by perverts and degenerates, and that it misportrayed the extent of liberalism's acceptance among common citizens.[16] A somewhat broader interpretation of this category would also lead us to include stories on declining support for Norman Lear, on the biases in Lear's television specials, and on the tendency of the media to attack both President Reagan and fundamentalists.[17]

The selection of issues in 1982 illustrated the point that the Moral Majority approached its agenda opportunistically. That is, the *Report* educated members about major social and moral issues only when there was a plausible tie-in to a story in the news. If there was no story worth reporting, then that element of the overall agenda was downplayed for that year. We see this illustrated in the apparent disappearance of coverage on pornography and on Israel: both were top-five stories in preceding years, and both were prominently featured in the official "What Is the Moral Majority?" pamphlet, yet neither warranted coverage in 1982. While we might claim that this disappearance reflected a major reshuffling of priorities away from these issues, this would not explain why they were not dropped from subsequent editions of the pamphlet or why the pornography issue reappeared so strongly later.

1983

While four of the top five issues on 1983's agenda had received substantial attention in the preceding years, 1983's top issue had not. That issue was national security, and its dominance of the 1983 agenda created a sharp contrast with 1982's nearly exclusive focus on domestic concerns. The subsidiary issues of 1983 were, in order: abortion, the unrest in Central America, school prayer, and homosexuality.

National security was, by far, the dominant issue of 1983. It amassed about 50 percent more coverage than the abortion issue and appeared in ten of the year's eleven issues of the *Report*.

Falwell recognized the fact that this priority represented a substantial shift in emphasis, and sought to allay members' fears that he had neglected the organization's traditional moral agenda. The *Report* noted that:

Concerned that some Moral Majority supporters may feel he is currently placing too much emphasis on defense-related issues, Dr. Falwell points out that in the four-year history of Moral Majority, he has emphasized the protection of unborn life, the return of voluntary prayer to public schools and other moral issues almost exclusively. Now, he believes grassroots Americans must face the truth that, unless America survives as a free nation, all other issues will become historically mute [sic]. "At the same time," said Falwell, "I do not intend to neglect support for the other issues."[18]

While this did represent a fairly radical shift in emphasis for the organization, Falwell used this same logic to explain his support for a strong defense in his book, *Listen, America!*[19]

In dealing with national security, the Moral Majority dealt primarily with three issues. The first, and largest, of these was the nuclear freeze, a call to halt all testing and deployment of new nuclear weapons systems. In 1983, the nuclear freeze movement had reached the apex of its visibility, and the Moral Majority chose to devote two cover stories to the freeze, calling it "the big lie" and declaring that we must "freeze the freeze."[20] The second issue concerned the construction of a space-based antiballistic missile system, which President Reagan referred to as his "Strategic Defense Initiative." Relying heavily on the expert advice of retired General Daniel Graham, the hawkish former leader of the Pentagon's Defense Intelligence Agency, the *Report* devoted one cover story and several internal ones to the need for defending ourselves from Soviet attack. The final, related issue was a general call for strengthening America's defenses and was issued under President Reagan's slogan of "Peace Through Strength."[21] While there were a number of other military issues, for example, a little coverage of the downing of Korean Air Lines flight 007 by the Soviets, these three issues clearly dominated.

Abortion continued to play a consistent second-fiddle; it was the Moral Majority's second most covered issue for the third year in a row. Coverage in 1983 was scattered over a range of abortion-related issues, including: the Hyde amendment to ban use of federal funds for abortion, the Hatch amendment to ban abortion, the tenth anniversary of the *Roe v. Wade* decision, and a variety of minor horror stories such as aborted fetuses being found in an incinerator. Unlike preceding years, the abortion coverage largely avoided both the generalized polemics on the sin of abortion and the extensive coverage of single issues, such as the Hatch and Helms proposals had received in the preceding year.

The third most important issue in 1983 was the accelerating unrest in Central America. While this issue was discussed in only four issues of the *Report*, its extensive coverage in September gave it a fairly large page total for the year. These articles focused mainly on two themes: the communist-supported aggression in Nicaragua, and the possibility that huge numbers of refugees would be created by the conflict and that they might be forced northward through Mexico toward the United States.[22]

The school-prayer issue was nearly tied with Central America for the third position. While school prayer continued to be the subject of some substantive discussion, the coverage was dominated by discussions of the reintroduced Hatch and Reagan amendments. The Hatch amendment called for accepting silent prayer in schools, while the Reagan amendment just called for prayer. More important than either, however, were a series of full-page entreaties-cum-advertisments by the Moral Majority calling for people to write their elected representatives and to send money to the Moral Majority. Since there were no comparable appeals related to any of the preceding issues, it seems that the Moral Majority was indicating a psychic investment that was out of proportion to the number of pages devoted to the issue.

Finally, the Moral Majority devoted some coverage to the gay community. In previous years, the organization concentrated on what it perceived as the general moral decrepitude of homosexuals but in 1983 focused coverage sharply on the emergence of the Acquired Immune Deficiency Syndrome (AIDS) in the gay community. The issue was considered explosive enough to warrant two cover stories, one with a photo depicting the average American family at risk and the other showing the word "AIDS" filling an outline of the United States.

There were, then, two interesting features to 1983's agenda. First, foreign affairs and national security became important for the first time. While Falwell had probably always been concerned with these issues, as evidenced by their inclusion in the "What Is the Moral Majority?" pamphlet's issue list, he had never before publicly recognized them in the *Report*. Second, this was the first year in which the issues were purely substantive. That is, each previous year featured significant coverage of administrative or legitimizing issues, of the type described in Chapter 3, but 1983 featured only issues of substance. This seemed to imply a growing confidence on the Moral Majority's part, a confidence that its place in the political system was now indisputable.

1984

The 1984 presidential election colored that year's Moral Majority agenda in two ways: first, coverage of the election campaign was the year's second-leading issue. Second, the Moral Majority's desire to influence the election led to the re-emergence of a significant number of mobilization appeals. The dominance of these two issues probably helped to explain abortion's decline to third rank and school prayer's drop to number five.

By a wide margin, the year's leading issue was attacks on church-related schools by state officials. The Nebraska church issues, which were so widely discussed in 1982, were the leading edge of a welter of these stories, which appeared in nine of eleven issues and were featured on three of the year's first five covers. As in 1982, these stories generally focused on the question of the right of the state to control curriculum at church schools; the states argued that they could and were willing to declare students at unapproved schools to be truants, and to arrest pastors who kept such institutions running. Unlike 1982, however, the churches were able to report substantial victories in 1984. In Nebraska, the state legislature passed a law that decreased state involvement in church schools by loosening certification standards. In Maine, a federal judge ruled that the state could not prosecute parents of children who were attending unapproved schools. Both measures passed by April, and subsequent coverage of the issue declined sharply.

As already mentioned, the second-leading issue was the 1984 elections. The Moral Majority's coverage began in mid-year, with Falwell's announced plans to attend both conventions. Later coverage included Falwell's reception at the convention, discussions of the nominees (particularly Geraldine Ferraro, the Democratic candidate for vice-president), summaries of the party platforms and a continuing indictment of the Democratic party. While the Moral Majority, technically, did not endorse candidates or tickets, its hints about proper voting were rarely subtle. The Reverend LaHaye, for example, asked:

Do we want to pay higher taxes so government can grow bigger and control more of our lives or do we want less government and more liberty? Do we want "peace through strength" by providing a strong national defense or do we want peace through weakness designed by those who believe we can trust the Communists to be "humane" (in spite of KAL-007 and Afghanistan)?[23]

In analyzing the two platforms, another article noted that the democrats wanted more government, that they cited Supreme Court rulings that "forbid prayer and devotional Bible reading," that they had no section on "the family," and that they "refuse to recognize the unborn child as a person."[24] Abortion, as we have noted, was the year's third most prominent issue; it appeared in seven of eleven issues and on one cover. Perhaps discouraged by Congress' repeated rejection of the various antiabortion initiatives, the Moral Majority's emphasis began to shift from condemning abortion to promoting alternatives. Thus, the cover story was on the Moral Majority's "Save-A-Baby" drive, which planned to eliminate 500,000 abortions yearly by establishing a thousand Save-A-Baby centers. These centers would "freely provide unwed pregnant women with housing, counseling, medical care, education and adoption."[25] In particular, Falwell seemed concerned that they "provide counseling for pregnant girls to offset the death-oriented propaganda of the abortion clinics."[26]

The mobilization appeals were also tied to the presidential elections. Rather than mimicking earlier years' appeals, which centered on getting people broadly involved in politics, 1984's appeals were more limited to getting them to register and vote. So, for example, the April issue had a cover story entitled "Moral Majority mobilizes huge voter-registration drive," with an accompanying full-page advertisement, on page nineteen, asking for financial support to launch "the most comprehensive voter registration campaign in our history!"[27] The organization's special election issue featured a cover story claiming that the Moral Majority had registered 8 million new voters, although it seems likely that this was a four-year total. The *Report* also claimed that the "Moral Majority has 20% of the electorate."[28] Combined with inner-page exhortations to "Get Out and Vote," and a story entitled, *"Destiny:* Our 1984 Imperative—We Go to the Polls on November 6,"[29] this suggested a strong commitment to the short-term objective of winning in November.

The Moral Majority again got its hopes up about passage of a school-prayer bill and, again, rationalized defeat. After front-page stories and full-page advertisements in March, the Moral Majority reported another defeat in May. Undaunted, it attributed the defeat to the blindness of elected officials who were unwilling to listen to the voice of the people. The bitterness of defeat was tempered, however, by the hope that an upcoming Supreme Court case and passage of the "equal access" bill, which allowed religious student groups to have access to school facilities on an equal basis with nonreligious groups, would still solve the problem.

This year's agenda seemed to reflect the Moral Majority's growing maturity and sense of perspective. Despite losing on a number of its issues, the Moral Majority continued to press toward a more hopeful future, rather than becoming shrill or disenchanted. Many of its claims were more pragmatic and less hortatory: they stressed the importance of voting rather than the need to become part of some "Christian army," and addressed the need for prayer in terms far less shrill than those used two years earlier. While the organization was still staunchly conservative, it seemed that the tenor of its conservatism was changing.

1985

The agenda of the Moral Majority's last year of existence was undistinguished. The organization was concerned with, in descending order, pornography, the quality of education, abortion, AIDS, and relations between church and state. Of these, only the concern with education was a newcomer to the top of the organization's agenda. Even this claim needs to be limited by remembering that the schools were integral to a number of major Moral Majority positions, such as school prayer and the acceptability of homosexual teachers.

There were several different themes embodied in the organization's coverage of the pornography issue. Predominant among these was the rising tide of grassroots successes: Cox Cable Company dropped "The Playboy Channel" in the Norfolk, Virginia, area; the American Civil Liberties Union supported the right of citizens to picket and boycott distributors of pornography; the Southland Corporation, parent body to the ubiquitous 7-11 Stores, was picketed and marched upon; 6,000 retail outlets ceased the sale of pornographic magazines over the first six months of 1985; dozens of local antipornography groups were formed, and so on. In addition to reporting these efforts, the Moral Majority encouraged them with primers on political activism and publicity. The second sort of coverage given to pornography was a recounting of its myriad forms. Readers were regaled with descriptions of pedophilia, sado-masochism, pornographic cable channels and video-cassettes, pornography via telephone and personal computer, pornographic rock lyrics, and the rise of "couples' films," which were nonsexist erotica, often produced by women, for the enjoyment of both men and women. In defense of the Moral Majority, we should note that these articles largely avoided the temptation to become lurid; indeed, several seemed reasonably even-handed in discussing the pornography industry and its audience.

Coverage of public education focused on two seemingly con-

tradictory themes: the ongoing improvement of public education and its utter depravity. Stories of the first sort occurred
earlier in the year and included Presient Reagan's paean to the
"back to the basics" movement, state initiatives to recruit new
teachers by circumventing schools of education and allowing
any college-educated person to take teaching certification tests,
federal laws that had been designed to prevent federal support
of courses that taught "secular humanist" values and the
appointment of the reassuringly conservative William Bennett
to be secretary of education. Around mid-year, the tone seemed
to shift away from this positive one with the rise of a number of
articles on the need for home schools, and in September, the
swing toward the negative was completed when the Moral
Majority devoted a substantial fraction of its *Report* to the influence of secular humanism on education, and to the horrors of
death education, anti-Americanism, and values clarification.
The issue was capped off by ritualistically reprinting sections of
the "Humanist Manifesto II," a popular bugaboo for the conservatives.[30]

Abortion, too, was covered through two distinct focuses. In
1985, the pro-life movement was suffering from a generational
schism. The older part of the movement stressed political action
and education. A younger cadre, impatient with the seeming
failures of their elders, stressed confrontation and violence. In
part, the *Report* covered the fringe successes of the antiabortion
movement: the Massachusetts Supreme Court ruled that a
drunken driver could be held guilty of murder for the death of a
fetus, the state of Colorado banned funding for abortions, the
state of Pennsylvania saw a decrease in the number of abortions
under a new law, one hospital in Maryland was petitioned by its
member-physicians to halt abortions, and the Supreme Court
was to hear cases that might limit the availability of abortions.
The greatest hope, though, was clearly invested in screenings of
the antiabortion documentary *The Silent Scream*, which was
narrated by one-time abortionist Bernard Nathanson and which
featured the images, captured by an ultrasound scanner, of a
fetus actually being aborted.

The extent of progress here was clearly not sufficient for the
Moral Majority or others in the pro-life camp. Its victories were

fragmentary, and its continued failures were permitting the execution of millions of unborn children annually. This strain had given rise to a violent wing in the pro-life movement, a wing that picketed and bombed abortion clinics. The Moral Majority seemed incapable of making a decisive judgment on these acts. On the one hand, the organization clearly stated that "we do not have the right to bomb abortion clinics" and labeled the acts "terroristic."[31] On the other hand, it noted that the bombers "behave like people would rationally be expected to behave if they really believed abortion was murder," and it ran a column by the unreconstructed Patrick Buchanan, who declared that abortionists were "the real terrorists."[32] While the organization officially held to the former position, it gave somewhat greater prominence to the latter.

The AIDS issue received greater prominence than in the past, but the Moral Majority remained oddly restrained in its coverage of the issue. The great majority of the space was devoted to detailing simply the spread of the disease and the limited hope held out by medical researchers for finding a timely cure. There was some discussion of the advent of laws designed to restrain transmission of the disease and of the particular threats to innocent hemophiliacs, but very little moralizing about homosexuality or divine retribution.

Finally, the *Report* devoted its fifth greatest amount of space to covering the continuing conflicts between church and state. By and large, this was a tale of continuing setbacks, since more evangelists were arrested for running unlicensed schools, more civil suits were filed for "clerical malpractice," and more courts, including the Supreme Court, turned their backs on the appeals of religionists. The year's one bright spot, a federal court ruling that upheld the constitutionality of the "Equal Access" law, which gave religious student organizations access to school facilities for after-school meetings, was tarnished by the continued failure of school administrators to take the act seriously.

In sum, then, the 1985 agenda was largely conventional and was a reasonable extension of the trends developed in the preceding three years. Even so, there were a few developments of note beyond the stress on these traditional issues. One was the rise of international and military issues in the organization's agenda. Issues such as the president's Strategic Defense Initiative, communism in Central America, and the Moral Majority's continuing efforts against starvation in Africa were among the top dozen covered by the *Report*, and their combined coverage about matched the space devoted to the organization's number-one issue, pornography. There were at least two international stories, however short, in each issue of the *Report* and three cover stories. This represents the most coverage ever given to international or security affairs.

A second interesting sidelight was the continued stress on lionizing the Reverend Falwell. The *Report* devoted three stories to detailing recognitions of the Reverend Falwell as one of America's most influential private citizens, most admired men, and as a newly inducted member of the National Religious Broadcaster's "Hall of Fame." At the same time, the organization continued to deride those who chose to disagree with it. Two former allies, the evangelical journal, *Christianity Today*, and conservative Congressman Mickey Edwards of Oklahoma were labeled as "having capitulated to the secular media . . . naive and biased" and as a "fading star," respectively.[33] The need to allocate space to such activities implies that the organization was not quite so secure as it would have had its readers believe.

We know, then, that the Moral Majority tended to address the same issues as the years went on. To the extent that new issues were addressed, they were logical extensions of the Moral Majority's core agenda. So, even though AIDS and the Strategic Defense Initiative were not elements of the organization's initial agenda, they were clearly related to central concerns: gay rights and national defense, respectively. What we need to do next is to examine the possibility that there were significant changes in the way the Moral Majority approached its comparatively stable agenda.

EVOLVING STRATEGIES IN CENTRAL ISSUES

The easiest way to understand changes within the organization's agenda is to look closely at a representative portion of the agenda. In this section, we will look at three key concerns of the Moral Majority: Christianity, abortion, and pornography. While Christianity was unlike abortion and pornography in the sense that it was not a discreet item on the organization's agenda, the issue was so important to the organization and to its critics that it requires specific attention.

Christianity

The Moral Majority recognized the sensitivity of this issue. As noted in Chapter 1, one of the most frequent charges against the Moral Majority was that it sought to create an American theocracy and to impose a single orthodoxy on all people.[34] The organization clearly distanced itself from any religious ties in the "What Is the Moral Majority?" pamphlet, and Falwell raised the stakes further when he claimed: "we must always prevent Moral Majority from becoming religious. In fact, the day it does, it will die."[35] In one widely reported statement in 1985, Falwell apologized for the insensitivity of many fundamentalists, and claimed that "this is not a Christian nation and clearly it should not be. We have been careless in our rhetoric."[36]

When we talk about Christianity as an issue, we are talking about the organization's self-image. The question is: to what extent does the Moral Majority implicitly portray itself as a religious organization? We can say that the organization is describing itself as religious when any one of a number of things occurs. It is religious if it describes its audience as religious. That is, when it talked of getting its members "out of the pews" or when it wanted "to emphasize [its point] to Christian Americans,"[37] it was defining itself differently than when it got "conservative Americans out of their seats." Similarly, the organization is religious if its strategies are religious. If the organization asked its members to "pray for our activities" and its various projects were its "ministries,"[38] it was defining itself differently than if its members were asked to "support our task forces." Finally, an organization is religious if the warrants for its claims are religious. When "the most important reason for Israel's survival [is that] Our Savior came from the Jewish family" or a new theory of evolution was refuted by proving that it was "as atheistic as ever,"[39] the organization was defining itself differently than a secular group that supported Israel because of its geopolitical importance or objected to the theory because of its nonfalsifiability.

These few examples, drawn mostly from the first issue of the *Report*, highlight the fact that if the Reverend Falwell's dire prophecy were true, then the organization would have been stillborn. As we noted in our discussion of the organization's early rhetoric, the Moral Majority de facto started as a religious organization: all of its national staff transferred over from the "Old-Time Gospel Hour," all of its state chairmen were fundamentalist ministers, its newspaper was just a renaming of Falwell's church newspaper, and its members were the members of his ministry.[40] A close look at the first issue of the *Report* shows the extent to which Christianity dominated the organization's psyche.

The cover of this first issue featured a story on prayer in the schools, claimed that "to stand against Israel is to stand against God," announced that 1 million church workers had been mobilized, and that an inside story would detail the role of Christians in politics. On page two, Governor James of Alabama declared a boycott of "conferences which do not establish traditional Judeo-Christian values." On page three, ministers were the ones shocked by Carter's school-prayer veto, and Falwell emphasized important points to "Christian Americans" and promised "every Christian pastor" a letter. The Domestic Violence bill, on page four, was derided because it was not "consistent with Bible morality." The article on page five was "a Christian physician" opposed to pornography. Page six explained that support for Israel was required because Jesus had been a Jew. On page eight, the *Report* explained that at the Moral Majority's first national convention "more than 2,000 pastors and Christian workers have endorsed a resolution to . . . involve the moral majority of Christian Americans in the political process." Charles Moore, the organization's national field director, explained on the next page "how each state can be organized to recruit Christians." On page ten, Texas textbook critic Norma Gabler attacked current texts for attacking Christian values. On page twelve, the Moral Majority strengthened its lobbying against a pending Criminal Code Revision by asking its members to "pray for our activities." Page fourteen contained a report of Falwell's appearance on a nationally syndicated television program, *The Donahue Show*. On that program, Falwell announced that "television must be used for Christ," described the Moral Majority as having "unique ministries," and claimed that "until recently, Christians have been a community in exile in the life of our country." The final two pages of the *Report* were devoted to the article, "Out of the Pew, Into the Precinct," which detailed "what Christians can do" and which was buttressed by four Bible quotations.

This emphasis cannot be explained away as the one-time excesses of novices publishing their first issue. The dominance of Christianity in identifying audience, argument, and tactic continued for months. The eleventh issue, for example, noted on its front cover that church attendance was high, opposed the promotion of "non-Christian" morality, asked "What is a Christian to do?" in relation to sex education, and exposed a conspiracy to undercut Christian values in America.[41]

The emphasis on Christianity, however, waned with time. As the number of references to Christianity dropped, the nature of the remaining references began to change. The term "Judeo-Christian" was invoked more frequently, and "religious" and "conservative" became the adjectives preferred to "Christian." At the same time, the *Report* began running more stories about other Protestants, Catholics, Jews, and Mormons who shared the Moral Majority's concerns.

By 1982, there was very little mention of Christianity, and religion was never more than the sanitized version offered by America's civil religion. In 1983 and 1984, there were fewer than a half-dozen references, and most of those were on the order of "God-fearing Americans."

In 1985, the last year of the organization's existence, the pendulum began to swing back. The *Report* remained largely secular, but a slowly growing body of changes started to blur the distinction between the Moral Majority and Falwell's fundamentalist church. The changes, taken separately, are innocuous. In April, the *Report* ran an anomalous story about a religious tour of Israel by Falwell and his followers. The article, entitled

"830 Enjoy Holy Land Tour," was reminiscent of a travel agent's advertising copy:

The combining of a deluxe tour of the Holy Land with elective experiences and travel options available with an international prophecy conference made *Israel '85* a unique experience, even for the seasoned Middle East traveler . . . the cost of experiencing *Israel '85* was three to five hundred dollars cheaper than many tours offering tour accommodations and less attractive options . . . Dr. Falwell provided tremendous evenings of spiritual ministry. Don Norman . . . brought the house down when he sang "Jerusalem" on the last evening.[42]

The *Report* had never before hyped one of Falwell's many religious ventures as news.

The same issue featured a story on a Falwell telecast from Israel, in which he decried anti-Semitism by Christians and the story of a Nicaraguan tortured by the Sandinistas. The interview with the Nicaraguan was arranged through "friends in the Christian community," and featured recollected dialogue in which Sandinista soldiers announced "pastors and preachers are our enemies."[43] In the paper's center, there were four short articles under "Reports from Headquarters." One noted that Falwell had addressed a prophecy conference, the second noted that Vice-President Godwin was overseeing the Liberty Education Network to "reach Christian schools nationwide," the third said that field director Mooneyham was warning of threats to Christian day care in North Carolina, and the fourth said that legislative director Jones had met with the Christian Education Association.[44] None of these articles made much fuss about the activities, and all of them cited other things that the individuals had been involved in; nevertheless, such a concentration of church-related activity was rare.

Small changes continued to accumulate. In May, the paid advertisement from Liberty University was changed from a separate, inserted section into an integral part of the paper, and Godwin, who had begun to use "Dr." before his name, contributed an article on "exciting news" about Liberty University's School of Lifelong Learning. The School's correspondence courses offered "good news for Christian adults [and] . . . for middle-aged and senior Christians."[45] This article continued the practice of presenting Falwell's church activities as news in the *Report*. The following issue reported on the risks faced by the hemophiliac child of a Liberty University faculty member. The article was suffused with references to the family's Christian convictions, faith in God, and dependence on prayer as a way of coping with the risk of their son contracting AIDS.[46] The same issue attacked a new theory of evolution as being "as atheistic as ever." Lane Lester, director of the Liberty University Center for Creation Studies, complained that the theory "has no more connection with the Scripture than any other evolutionary hypothesis." The article goes on to explain that the Bible "doesn't say man was made out of clay, but out of the elements of the earth."[47]

The sum of these changes does not nearly return the *Report* to the high degree of religious involvement evident in its earliest issues. The changes do indicate a heightened sensitivity to the interests of a Christian audience and may reflect an act of retrenching that was a prelude to the far more radical changes by the organization's conversion from the Moral Majority to the Liberty Federation in the beginning of the next year. In any case, the changes do reflect a rebound from the extremely secular and purely political focus of the organization's middle years to a more determinedly Christian and religious emphasis in its twilight

Abortion

Abortion was one of the Moral Majority's central issues. While it did not always top a given year's agenda, it always was among the most significant items and was the most visible one. While the organization always abominated abortion, the strategies of its opposition changed over time.

Initially, the Moral Majority focused on the horrors of the abortion trade. In the first issue of the *Report*, for instance, a "distinguished black physician" posited a slippery slope from "the continuing murder of millions of babies every year" to "tomorrow [when] it could be the elderly or sickly people or even those who have different views." Almost as bad was the

fact that abortion allowed women to shirk their "primary obliga-
tion to propagate our humankind."[48] Other articles described
abortion as a "moral cancer disguised as 'a woman's right to
choose'" and the women who applied to Planned Parenthood
as "women who want, but can't afford to kill their babies."[49]

This emphasis on graphic description and evaluation continued
for several years. In 1981, for instance, the Moral Majority coined
the term "biological holocaust" to describe the 1.5 million
abortions that occurred annually. That same year, they also
claimed that Planned Parenthood had a "genocide packet," and
that black leaders called abortion genocide.[50] An article by
fundamentalist philosopher Francis Schaeffer, entitled "Abortion: Death Stench Becomes Distant," compared abortion to
every act of mass murder that came to the author's mind:
pogroms, the murder of slaves in the antebellum South, the
Nazi death camps, and attacks by B-52 bombers.[51] The typical
appeal was for prayers that "our leader's ears will be sensitive
to the haunting cries of butchered children."[52]

As we noted in the preceding section, coverage in the Moral
Majority's middle years (1982-83) focused mainly on the
vicissitudes of the legislative process. Each new initiative was
greeted with the enthusiasm reflected in the 1982 title: "Finally,
a Chance to Stop Abortion."[53] Each successive defeat was
recorded on the inner pages of the *Report*.

By 1984, however, the Moral Majority departed radically from
its earlier positions. As mentioned earlier, in January of that
year, Falwell launched his "Save-a-Baby" ministry. The Save-a-
Baby drive created residential centers around the country in
which pregnant women could enroll; they would receive housing, education, counseling, food and medical care. In return,
they pledged not to have an abortion, and the center offered
licensed adoption services for any mother who still felt unwilling to keep her child. The idea was that abortions often occurred
because the potential mother felt that she was not ready to be a
parent or was incapable of supporting a child. The Save-a-Baby
drive tried to blunt this justification by offering pregnant
women an alternative.

This represented a significant departure for several reasons.
First, it created a sense of accomplishment to counterbalance the

pro-life movement's continuing political losses. Second, it gave the Moral Majority something to argue for, rather than merely something to argue against. It would no longer just have to curse the darkness or be at the mercy of the argument that these poor women had no choice in the matter. Third, there was a corresponding change in the organization's attitude toward the women involved. While the 1980 articles described them as women who wanted to kill their babies, in 1984 they were girls facing "this awkward crisis" and, later, women "facing difficult circumstances."[54] One article even provided cheery case studies of five women in Save-a-Baby homes, one of whom was described as "bright, spunky, brown-eyed."[55]

To an extent, the organization tried to extend this positive perspective into 1985, but was thwarted by the growing schism in the pro-life movement. Falwell's hope was to create 1,000 centers over the next five years, with the prospect of eliminating one-third of all abortions.[56] Unfortunately, many people were not satisfied either with the limited effects of such positive incentives or with the negligible gains generated by the political system. These were people who increasingly took their protests to the streets and who backed their complaints with "the propaganda of the act."[57] A wave of picketing and bombings generated national attention.

Falwell was marvelously indecisive in the face of this crisis. As already noted, the Moral Majority made a half-hearted, nearly pro forma denunciation of the bombings at the same time as it ran a series of articles that implicitly condoned them. In some instances, the same article would sympathetically review the bombers' reasoning while deploring their acts. Falwell himself had difficulty even enunciating a clear position on whether he opposed all abortions. Thus, Falwell said one week that he would oppose a law that made all abortions illegal because he felt that abortions were justified whenever the mother's life was threatened. The next month, he said that he was praying for the day when all abortions would be illegal, and still later, said that he would like all abortions to be illegal but would accept a law that made a number of compromises on the issue.[58] Falwell then spent nearly a month trying to extricate himself from these seemingly inconsistent positions.

Over time, then, the Moral Majority's arguments about abortion changed in several noteworthy ways. First, it became noticeably less angry and negative. The number of stories about incinerated fetuses and botched abortions dwindled with time, until finally the issue was discussed without the intrusion of the earlier images. Second, it became more innovative and flexible in its responses to the crisis. In addition to strong lobbying, the organization started its Save-a-Baby drive and encouraged others to do likewise. This also reflected changed attitudes toward the women involved from being callous criminals to being choiceless victims. The Reverend Falwell's occasionally unclear pronouncements on abortion also, at base, reflected a reasonable degree of pragmatism. Even though Falwell considered abortion to be murder, he expressed a willingness to permit a small number of abortions to continue as the price for eliminating the great majority of them. Thus, he supported bills that would still permit abortion in the cases of rape, incest, and danger to the mother even though he felt that the first two categories were spurious. Finally, the articles themselves switched from being angry polemics written by outsiders to being largely reportorial pieces authored by members of the *Report* staff. Presumably, this gave the organization greater control over both the timing and the substance of its agenda.

Pornography

Our look at Christianity and abortion established the Moral Majority's pattern of argument. It began with a simple position, replete with clear good-versus-evil dichotomies and ample atrocity stories. Ultimately, its position recognized shades of gray: "baby killers" became "girls in trouble." These changes did not signal a change in principles, but rather in its tactics. The attacks became less rabid, and the solutions more complex. This same general pattern was repeated in the case of pornography, a central moral issue.

The early rhetoric surrounding pornography was among the Moral Majority's most hysterical. In the first issue of the *Report*, former Olympic medalist Gary Hall recited the dangers of pornography, which included "several studies" that proved that "70-80% of sexually related crimes are inspired by pornography." The capstone of Hall's article was the story of a band of twelve- and thirteen-year-old children who acquired a video-cassette player and a pornographic tape that depicted "every type of perversion imaginable." As Mr. Hall explained: "After the initial embarrassment, the majority of the kids were completely seduced. They stripped their clothes and attempted to outdo the adults right then and there."[59] As a result, one youngster had headaches for four years, became impotent, jaded, dependent on drugs for sexual release, and incapable of idealized love.

About the same tack was taken in July of 1980 by an article in the *Report* that presented historical and anthropological studies on the effects of pornography. According to the *Report*, "Dobson [one of Falwell's assistant pastors] cited a study of 2,000 cultures, 55 of which were characterized by sexual ambiguity or no distinct sex roles. 'Not one of those 55 cultures has survived,' he said."[60]

The same story cited another study of eighty civilizations that showed "a sexual pattern of life and death in those civilizations." Another article cited the work of seven professors who suggested that the changes wrought by pornography could cause the collapse of civilization.[61]

The most radical expression of these fears was presented in an article reprinted from the February, 1981, issue of *War on Drugs*.[62] The unnamed authors of the article argued that:

Porn and dope have been spread among our society by the same network of individuals, who refer to their collective efforts as "the Aquarian Conspiracy." Their ultimate aim is the creation of a "postindustrial society," a commitment to reversing scientific progress and returning to a new dark age. The architects of this policy were H.G. Wells, Lord Bertrand Russell, Aldous and Julian Huxley, George Orwell and Margaret Mead, among others.

The article then implied that radical action was needed.

From this inauspicious beginning, though, the Moral Majority developed its most pragmatic campaign. Rather than focusing on the need for national laws, the great majority of articles discussed private collective actions. The *Report* presented a veritable "how-to" guide on organizing and publicizing boycotts and demonstrations. It also presented a steady stream of updates on the successes of the antipornography crusade. At the same time, its ran few "horror stories." The popularity and success of its private actions probably made such stories unnecessary.

In 1985, the *Report* presented a flurry of stories explaining pornography's many forms: "x-rated video cassettes, telephone sex services, erotic satellite and cable movies and now sex via computer."[63] However, even these stories were curiously restrained. While there was clear disapproval of all of this, there were no really seething condemnations. For example, one article quoted Al Goldstein, publisher of *Screw* magazine, as saying, "Maybe the religious right will now realize that they are doomed—doomed for fighting the battle of evil and repression."[64] Significantly, the *Report* did not use any disparaging labels to describe Mr. Goldstein or the other pornographers quoted. In an earlier year, Goldstein would have inevitably been assigned a sobriquet, such as "smut king" or "porn pusher." Further, the Moral Majority did not feel compelled to respond to Goldstein's allegation. It simply reported it and then went on to discuss some of the aspects of the new technology of pornography. The article also described the rise of "couple's films," which were erotic films designed to appeal to married couples rather than the prototypical "raincoat crowd." This section seemed to imply the possibility of legitimate erotica.

Even articles on sado-masochism and pedophilia were more descriptive than damning. The *Report* article on sado-masochism clearly described the contents of such films, but it also carried out an extensive dialogue with the producers and performers of "legitimate" adult films. The article noted that most of these people tried to distance themselves from the makers of sado-masochistic films and also noted that most of the people interviewed were strongly critical of these films. The article itself did not condemn nonviolent pornography and even presented the film-makers' justifications for their art. Even the article's conclusion was singularly measured:

Actually, the Constitution protects pornography as long as community standards allow its existence. And the question before the porn industry is: How long will community standards tolerate the irresponsible depiction of child sex and violent acts against women? The answer to this question will also be the answer to the question of how long the Constitution will continue to protect pornography—something the pornographers should think about.[65]

Similarly, the article on pedophilia did nothing more than list the five ways in which child pornography serves the pedophile. The article did not explicitly rail against these people, did not assign any labels to them, and ended with the simple injunction, "Pray for these children."[66]

In sum, the Moral Majority's position on pornography had matured considerably. Even while instructing members on how to eliminate all pornography from their communities, the Moral Majority became less intent on proving that pornography would lead to the downfall of the Western world. It implied that all pornography was not equally offensive and even, to a degree, legitimated "adult entertainment."

It seems that historian Frances Fitzgerald was right when she observed that, "Falwell's own politics did not change very much,"[67] when one compares his agenda for 1981 with his agenda for 1986. The body of issues that the Moral Majority chose to address remained reasonably consistent: national defense, abortion, pornography, school prayer, gay rights, and the Equal Rights Amendment. Different issues were dominant in different years, but the basic list changed little.

The changes that did occur were, however, important. The attacks on the Moral Majority always centered more on its means than on its ends, and the greatest changes occurred in those means. The Moral Majority's allegations became less overwrought, its targets were more clearly defined, and its worldview became less Manichean. Defeats were no longer total defeats, and victories no longer needed to be total victories. This reflected a greater degree of political maturity and of confidence about its place in the political arena. It became one more player in a pluralist game. In part, then, we can conclude that much of the significant change on the issues was a change in style. We will pursue this finding in the following chapter.

NOTES

1. Jerry Falwell, "An Interview with the Lone Ranger of American Fundamentalism," *Christianity Today*, 4 September 1981, p. 1099.

2. Robert Billings, "Out of the Pew, Into the Precincts," *Moral Majority Report*, 14 March 1980, p. 15. Hereafter cited as *Report*.

3. The *Report* organized its stories into eight categories: Politics and Government, National Security, Morality, Education, Economics, Human Life, Inside Moral Majority, and The Rest of the News. Since the Moral Majority found these categories adequate, it seemed reasonable to adopt them with a minor modification: a "Personalities" category was added to deal with a variety of stories that detailed the life and accomplishments of exemplary conservatives, such as Phyllis Schlafly, Edith Schaeffer, and Jack Kemp.

4. "Negative Government Acts" included all indictments of government action that were specific to individual policies, as opposed to dealing with the general folly of government. Examples included opposing revisions in the federal criminal code or rejecting a new domestic violence bill. "Our Enemies" covered the stories about the perfidious acts of individual liberals, as well as chronicling attacks on the Moral Majority and like-minded organizations by the media and other critics. "Contested Ground" dealt with all of those issues the Moral Majority had to judge on a case-by-case basis, such as court decisions and election results.

5. These estimates are based on computerized searches of the *National Newspaper Index* and *National Magazine Index* databases.

6. These were, for example, not covered in the "What Is the Moral Majority?" pamphlet.

7. *Report*, 24 May 1982. "Reagan's Amendment: The Nation Welcomes Plan to Restore Public School Prayer," cover and pp. 3-4; Patrick Buchanan, "History, Jurists Support Prayer in Public Places," pp. 4-5; Cal Thomas, "Without Prayer, Crime Up," p. 4; Alfred Balitzer, "School Prayer: Tradition Extended," pp. 5, 12-13.

8. Buchanan, "History, Jurists," p. 4; Balitzer, "School Prayer," p. 5.

9. Thomas, "Without Prayer," p. 4.

10. Ronald Godwin, "Symbols Wear Thin," *Report*, August 1982, p. 3; "Reagan: School Prayer Ban Is an Outrage," *Report*, October 1982, pp. 4, 13.

11. Douglas Johnson, "Filibuster Kills Pro-Life Bill," *Report*, October 1982, pp. 6-7.

12. "Nebraska Jails Pastor: A Shocking Story," *Report*, October 1982, pp. 3, 14; "The York Raid: Another School Raided," *Report*, October 1982, pp. 3, 14.

13. "The York Raid," p. 14.

14. Ronald Godwin, "Time for Fundamentalists Change, Face the Hard Choices," *Report*, November 1982, p. 15.

15. "Idaho Federal Judge Rules ERA Dead," *Report*, 25 January 1982, cover and p. 5; "Three States Kill ERA, Finally," *Report*, 28 June 1982, pp. 6, 9.

16. *Report*, 22 February 1982, "Reagan, Public Agree, Too Much Sex on TV," p. 6; "Stein: Is Hollywood a Mirror of the Left?" p. 9; "Do Broadcasters Show America?" p. 10.

17. "Why Reagan, Moral Majority Are Mistreated by National Media," *Report*, 15 January 1982, pp. 6-7; "Lear Finds No Room in the Hall," *Report*, 25 January 1982, p. 13; "Lear's Ratings Begin to Slip," *Report*, September 1982, p. 6.

18. "Falwell Plans to Double Moral Majority," *Report*, July 1983, p. 5.

19. Jerry Falwell, *Listen, America!* (New York: Doubleday, 1980).

20. "Nuclear Freeze: The Big Lie," *Report*, April 1983, cover and pp. 2-3, 10-11; "Freezing the Freeze," *Report*, April 1983, cover and pp. 2-3.

21. "Peace Through Strength," *Report*, April 1983, pp. 2-3; "George Bush Stands for Peace Through Strength," *Report*, May 1983, cover and p.2.

22. These are referred to as the "feet people," in evocation of the "boat people" who fled communist-ruled Vietnam in the 1970s.

23. Tim LaHaye, "Will Nation's 'Day of Destiny' See You at the Polls?" *Report*, November 1984, pp. 6, 19.

24. "Party Platforms Give 1984 Voters a Clear Choice," *Report*, November 1984, pp. 4, 22.

25. "MM Pledges to Support 'Save-a-Baby' Drive," *Report*, June 1984, cover and p. 3.

26. Jerry Falwell, quoted in "MM Pledges," p. 3.

27. "Moral Majority Mobilizes Huge Voter Registration Drive," *Report*, April 1984, cover.

28. "Liberals Enraged as MM Registers Millions," *Report*, November 1984, cover and p. 2; "Pollster Harris Says: Moral Majority has 20% of Electorate," *Report*, November 1984, cover.

29. "*Destiny:* Our 1984 Imperative—We Go to the Polls on November 6," *Report*, November 1984, p. 19.

30. The "Humanist Manifesto II" was signed on August 23, 1973 by a group of 120 prominent scientists and authors. The thrust of the document was to reaffirm faith in human intellect and progress, and called for, among other things, increased individual freedoms, recognition of the right to abortion, rights for homosexuals, universal education, world law, and global planning. With regard to religion, the Manifesto declared that: "No deity will save us, we must save

outselves" and that "traditional theism . . . is an unproved and outmoded faith."

Those people seeking to prove that secular humanism is either the state religion of the United States or that secular humanists are in control of the world rely heavily on the Manifesto. One Moral Majority cartoon, entitled "The Liberal Stereotype," exemplified this claim. The cartoon depicted a Norman Lear-like figure chained to a stuffed monkey, sporting "gay power" and "ERA" buttons, wearing rose-colored glasses and a collection of booklets on abortion, welfare, "ACLU mouthpiece[s]," and "how to break up patriotic and pro-moral rallies with loud abusive language." The figure was standing on copies of the "Humanist Manifesto" and "Humanist Manifesto II," which were "the foundation on which he stands." *Report*, 25 January 1982, p. 5.

Discussions of and excerpts from the "Manifesto" are in "The Right's New Bogyman," *Newsweek*, 6 July 1981, pp. 48-49, and Leo Rosten, *Religions of America* (New York: Simon and Schuster, 1975), pp. 542-544.

31. "1985: The Year Conservatives Lose Their Rose-Colored Glasses," *Report*, February 1985, p. 17.

32. "Will the Real Terrorists Please Stand Up," *Report*, February 1985, p. 2.

33. "ACU's Faded Star," *Report*, January 1985, p. 19.

34. Refer to the text surrounding notes 3-7 in Chapter 1.

35. "The Nutshell Interview: Jerry Falwell," *Nutshell*, 1981/1982, p. 41. *Nutshell* is an undated, unnumbered periodical distributed free on college campuses, primarily for the purpose of advertising. This issue was current on the University of Massachusetts' campus in December of 1981 and January of 1982.

36. "Falwell Attempts to Mend Inter-faith Fences," *Washington Post*, 4 April 1985. This article lacks a page number because it was obtained through the Moral Majority archives, whose clipping service does not save page numbers.

37. "Ministers Shocked: Carter Says He Will Veto Bill to Restore Prayer in Public Schools," *Report*, 14 March 1980, p. 3.

38. "Speaking Up," *Report*, 14 March 1980, p. 14.

39. "Falwell Says America Must Support Israel," *Report*, 14 March 1980, p. 7; "New Evolution Theory Tries 'Clay' This Time," *Report*, June 1985, p. 24.

40. This was discussed in Chapter 2, particularly in the section entitled, "Founding the Moral Majority: Variant Versions."

41. "Whatever Happened to Our Values?" *Report*, 15 August 1980, pp. 8-9; "Bagnal seeks North Carolina Seat in 5th District," *Report*, 15 August 1980, p. 10.

42. "830 Enjoy Holy Land Tour," *Report*, April 1985, p. 3.

43. "Nicaraguan Tortured by Sandinistas Tells Story," *Report*, April 1985, p. 4.

44. "The Moral Majority Reports . . . from Headquarters," *Report*, April 1985, p. 11.

45. Ronald Godwin, "School of Lifelong Learning Means Good News," *Report*, May 1985, p. 15.

46. Dennis Shumaker, "Bryan's Right to Life Supercedes Any Gay's Right to Privacy," *Report*, June 1985, p. 4.

47. "New Evolution Theory," p. 24.

48. "Distinguished Black Physician Opposes Legalized Abortion," *Report*, 14 March 1980, p. 4.

49. "Planned Parenthood: A Euphemism for Abortion on Demand," *Report*, 17 November 1980, p. 11; "No Federal Abortions: The High Court," *Report*, 14 July 1980, p. 14.

50. "Sickening Disrespect for Human Life," *Report*, 18 May 1981, p. 9; "Probe Shows Suppository Tests on Blacks," *Report*, 24 August 1981, p. 4.

51. "Abortion Death-Stench Becomes Distant," *Report*, 21 September 1981, p. 11.

52. "Sickening Disrespect," p. 9.

53. "Finally, A Chance to Stop Abortion," *Report*, September 1982, cover.

54. Janet Buffington, "Pregnancy Programs Offer Unwed Mothers Housing, Love," *Report*, January 1984, p. 16; "America Finally Hears the 'Silent Scream,'" *Report*, April 1985, p. 16.

55. Buffington, "Pregnancy Programs," p. 16.

56. "Save-a-Baby Reaches Out to Unborn Nationwide," *Report*, April 1984, supplement p. 1.

57. This was the term used by early twentieth-century anarchists who believed that the masses could be brought to accept anarchist ideals and that they could best be mobilized by dramatic, violent acts. They, therefore, denigrated the "propaganda of the word" in favor of the "propaganda of the act." Barbara Tuchman, *The Proud Tower: A Portrait of the World Before the War, 1890-1914* (New York: MacMillan, 1966).

58. Falwell's comments seemed directly contradictory. For example, "I, for one, would be opposed to such an all-inclusive amendment. I think the life of the mother is a justified exception for abortion." "Republican's Hold on Power Tenuous, Falwell Says," *New York Tribune*, 15 January 1985, archival article. Compare that with, "It is my earnest prayer that *all* abortions will be illegal very soon," *San Diego Tribune*, 23 February 1985, archival article. The next month, a Tucson newspaper reported Falwell as saying that the Moral Majority "still would favor abortions in cases of rape and incest," *Tucson Citizen*, 22

March 1985, archival article. That same month, the Moral Majority tried to clarify its position by distinguishing Falwell's "theological" opposition with his "political" acceptance. "Letter from America," *Report*, 18 March 1985, p. 14.

59. "Olympic Star Speaks Against Pornography," *Report*, 18 March 1980, p. 5.

60. "Unchecked Sexual Freedom Leads to Inevitable Decay of America," *Report*, 30 July 1980, p. 11.

61. "Citizens Can Stop Smut Peddlers, Says CDL," *Report*, 30 July 1980, p. 13. "CDL" is a conservative antipornography group, Citizens for Decency through Literature.

62. "How the Porn Industry Set Up the Dope Lobby," *Report*, 16 March 1981, p. 19.

63. "Porn Leaders Use High Tech to Unlock Livingroom Doors," *Report*, August 1985, pp. 2, 5.

64. "Porn Leaders," p. 2.

65. "Porn Industry Puts Public to the Test," *Report*, August 1985, p. 4.

66. "Pedophiles: They Call Their World a Better Place," *Report*, June 1985, p. 17.

67. Frances Fitzgerald, *Cities on a Hill* (New York: Simon & Schuster, 1986), p. 191.

Chapter Five

The Moral Majority and the War Metaphor

I'm playing offense all the time. I try to set the agenda, try to start most of the wars myself.

Jerry Falwell, 12 November 1982[1]

Though Falwell frequently makes allusions to sports, it is the military analogy that is central to his view of the church and its role in the world. [He has said], "The church should be a disciplined, charging army . . . Christians, like slaves and soldiers, ask no questions."

Frances Fitzgerald, 18 May 1981[2]

In the final section of Chapter 4, we examined the changes in the way the Moral Majority discussed Christianity, abortion, and pornography. That examination led to the conclusion that the Moral Majority's rhetorical style had changed: it was less combative, more understanding, and carefully qualified.

In this chapter, we will look at the Moral Majority's use of the war metaphor to describe its relationship with the secular world. By looking at all of the war-related images over the organization's six-year history, we will be able to test the conclusions that we drew in Chapter 4 by seeing whether they apply to the rest of the organization's concerns.

Our first task here is to review some of the issues surrounding metaphors, so we can better assess the significance of the changes we find. Since our main concern is with the Moral Majority, rather than with metaphors per se, it will be sufficient just to make a broad overview of the salient issues and not try to resolve any of the ongoing controversies among the various theories of metaphor use. Our second task will be largely descriptive. We will establish the nature of Falwell's war, and comment on its nature and ultimate decline. Our third and final undertaking will be to analyze the war to understand its genesis and decline, and the failure of competing metaphors to gain notoriety.

THE BASICS OF METAPHOR

A metaphor is a trope, or figure of speech, that functions by taking a word or phrase usually applied to one object and applying it, instead, to a completely different object. So, for example, we might refer to a president of the United States as "the mighty helmsman." In theory, this use of the metaphor leads us to impute certain qualities of a "mighty helmsman" onto the president. It implies that he knows where he is going and has the ability, the control over the helm, to get us there. This trope is related to, but more forceful than, the simile. A simile would be phrased: "the president is like a mighty helmsman." We have, at least since the time of Aristotle, viewed this as a less potent phrasing. Aristotle said that "because it is longer it is less attractive. Besides, it does not say outright that 'this' is 'that,' and therefore the hearer is less interested in the idea." This passage may be the genesis of Kenneth Burke's definition of metaphor as "a device for seeing something in terms of something else [which] brings out the thisness of a that, or the thatness of a this."[3]

Metaphors "work" by creating a problem for those who encounter them, because we find familiar words in unfamiliar settings. Our job, then, is to understand the implications of this transposition of terms. Metaphors, Aristotle explained, imply riddles.[4] A typical explanation suggests that our reaction to encountering a new metaphor is organized into three phases: first, we reject the metaphor because we think there is something wrong with the way the language is being used. Second, we attempt to understand what might have led to this particular use of words by listing the similarities that might serve as a basis for the metaphor's comparison. Finally, we comprehend the metaphor and gain some new insight from the incongruous combination.[5] In theory, "solving" the metaphor, like solving any puzzle, should provide us with a feeling of satisfaction and achievement. This serves the rhetor's purposes by getting the audience actively involved in deciphering the world in terms set by the rhetor.

This observation is important, first, because of the notion of an "energy transfer," which is engendered by the metaphor. The basic idea is that we are apt to be much more taken with, and protective of, ideas embodied in good metaphors. This is because we had to struggle to bring this knowledge into being, and our feelings of involvement and achievement lead us to treasure these products. Again, Aristotle provided a clear explanation: "words express ideas, and therefore those words are most agreeable that enable us to get hold of new ideas. Now strange words simply puzzle us; ordinary words convey only what we know already; it is from metaphor that we can best get hold of something fresh." David Sapir and Christopher Crocker provide a somewhat different translation of the same passage: "Midway between the unintelligible and the commonplace, it is a metaphor which most produces knowledge."[6]

Many scholars phrase this process of discovery in terms of the transfer, or creation, of energy. Hermann Stelzner spoke of the "potencies" and the "emotional and compelling power" of an apt metaphor. Martin Foss claimed that the core of a good metaphor is its "energy-tension," and Philip Wheelwright, similarly, claimed that "the essence of metaphor consists in a semantic tension." Earl MacCormac argued that "confronting a new vibrant metaphor produces an emotional tension in the hearer," and Jane Blankenship noted that "metaphor makes both the speaker and the listener work; both must resolve the tension implicit in the metaphor."[7] All of these terms, "power," "energy," "tension" (defined as "a kind of force"), "vibrant," and "work" (in physics, the product of applied energy), imply that a metaphor has the capacity to change those who perceive it.

Metaphors do not, however, last forever. Since this "energetic" function seems to be a key element of metaphor, we may say that an expression that has lost its ability to excite has lost its metaphorical character. Such a phrase will not necessarily pass out of common usage, but may simply become part of the everyday, literal elements of the language. This process, called "the literalization of metaphor," is represented by such literal, but once metaphorical, expressions as the leg of a table, the wing of an airplane, or the arm of a chair. These expressions may be called "dead metaphors" or just "literal language."[8]

The recognition that metaphors can "die" and, thereby, lose their energy is particularly important to us. Both common experience and the testimony of authorities assure us that metaphors are very powerful elements of speech. A good metaphor is, presumably, a device that will have great persuasive power. Moreover, critics can gain interesting insights into the mind of the metaphor's creator by examining the metaphor. A new, vibrant, tensive metaphor implies the presence of a powerful and creative intellect behind it. A dead metaphor, contrarily, is no more apt to excite an audience than any other clichè. A speaker dependent on dead metaphors betrays a mind that is either incapable of or unwilling to use the creative power of language. The difference between a live versus a dead metaphor may be important. For example, if the war metaphor is live, then it may influence the ways in which the Moral Majority perceives the world and understands its options. It might, for instance, make political compromise more difficult if the Moral Majority would normally consider compromise in wartime to be disloyal or treasonous. If the metaphor is dead, then it has passed into conventional language and probably carries no great significance for its users.

Unfortunately, a dead metaphor looks just like a live one and an incautious critic may not accurately judge whether a particular metaphor is dead to a particular audience. The most obvious way of determining whether a particular metaphor has died would be Aristotelean; that is, we would try to observe the effects of the metaphor on the audience. Unfortunately, this is not practical since Falwell's audience is huge and amorphous, and since there is, as Edwin Black has argued, no way of establishing a cause-effect chain between a given rhetorical act and an observed action.[9] An alternative method was suggested by Wayne Booth, who proposed a short list of criteria for determining whether a metaphor is effective. Booth's list, which he claimed "one could dig out of almost any rhetoric text from Aristotle to Whately," included:

1. Good metaphors of this kind are *active*, lending the energy of animated things to whatever is less energetic or more abstract. . . .
2. Good weapon metaphors are *concise*. . . .
3. Good metaphors are *appropriate*, in their grandeur or triviality, to the task in hand. . . .
4. It must be properly *accommodated to the audience*. . . .
5. Finally, such a metaphor should build a proper *ethos* for the speaker, building or sustaining his character as someone to be trusted.[10]

We shall return to a consideration of these criteria after we have had a chance to look at the nature and scope of Falwell's war.

We began our discussion of this section with the argument that "solving" a metaphor creates a sense of exhilaration, and that this observation was important for two reasons. Our first reason, just presented, was that metaphoric language can "energize" an idea much more effectively than literal language can. Our second reason is that metaphor may transcend the task of describing reality and ascend to the level of influencing the creation of reality.

The power of metaphors to influence the creation of reality seems grounded in their felicity as a device for organizing experience into clear and manageable packages. This observation derives from contemporary theories about the way that our brain processes reality. It was once thought that the brain was a kind of camera that indiscriminately and accurately perceived and recorded all occurrences within the reach of our senses.[11] This description was consistent with a widely held mechanical metaphor that was invoked to describe the workings of the universe, and it implies that we should be able to retrieve any particular "photograph" from our "archives" in order to allow an accurate reconstruction of reality. If this were the case, metaphors would not be particularly important, since people could always go back later to their "files" and test of the accuracy of the metaphor against their stored bits of reality.

Scientists now believe that the brain is far more selective in deciding which potential stimuli will actually be attended to. Because of this, we are forced to rely on conventions that let us understand what has passed and that allow us to make some type of prediction about what is coming. By organizing stimuli into familiar forms and by dismissing other stimuli as irrelevant, we free the remainder of our intellects for dealing with the unexpected, novel, or threatening. So, for instance, we can quickly decide that stimulus "X" represents a car rather than a mysterious agglomeration of steel, glass, and rubber, and that stimulus "Y" can be ignored since it is irrelevant to us. Metaphors fit into this general cognitive structure by providing a way for structuring, interpreting, and reacting to new situations by equating them with older, more familiar ones. The act of equating then allows the brain to apply pre-existing forms concerning appropriate responses to this situation, rather than being required to expend the energy to create whole new sets of behaviors. In short, we learn what behaviors work, and we continue to use this conventional wisdom unless we are confronted with some catastrophic challenge to our beliefs. The easiest illustration of this is our tendency to substitute a reliance on stereotypes for case-by-case evaluations of, for instance, atheists, fundamentalists, Jews, or whomever.

This means that metaphors are not mere ornaments added to a discourse, but are a fundamental way by which we define the social reality to which we choose to react. This position remains valid whether we claim that metaphors are a generative device by which we shape reality or merely serve to help direct our limited attention toward certain elements of reality and away from others.[12]

A number of scholars have expressed grave concerns about the ability of metaphor to shape our perceptions inaccurately. One study, by historian William Leuchtenberg, looked at the prevalence of the "war analog" in describing the Great Depression. After giving some 140 examples of the use of war imagery to describe the Depression, its causes, effects, and solutions, Leuchtenberg reached the conclusion that this language might actually have prolonged the Depression by misdirecting our attention. As one example, he claimed that the decision to grant business executives the rank of "general" led us away from an examination of the possibility that our generals were actually a cause of the war. Their rhetorical title, Leuchtenberg argued, made them immune to the analysis that might have led us to conclude that distorted business investment patterns actually lay at the heart of the Depression. His final judgment was that, while the war metaphor may have helped to organize collective action, it ultimately misled reformers and proved to be, in many ways, "treacherous."[13]

Other scholarship in this tradition included the discussion of the war metaphor in argumentation by Stelzner and Lakoff and Johnson.[14] Both studies noted that we tend to discuss argument in war terms: we attack and defend, we have opponents and losses, strategies and fall-back positions. All three writers express concern about the possibility that the prevalence of war imagery skews our understanding of the process of argumentation and debate. Stelzner, for example, ended his article with a list of questions about the implications of our metaphors for diverting our attention from particular perspectives. Lakoff and Johnson claimed that "the fact that we in part conceptualize arguments in terms of battle systematically influences the shape arguments take and the way we talk about what we do in arguing . . . it structures the actions we perform in arguing."[15]

A number of other studies also address the possibility that metaphor seriously distracts attention. Political scientist William Leogrande strongly objected to the use of the domino metaphor in describing conditions in Central America. Leogrande's contention is that the domino metaphor biases American foreign policy by creating a series of unproven assumptions. For example, the fall of dominoes occurs only upon outside intervention, and Leogrande argued that this forced us into the unexamined assumption that there must be outside influences in Central America, as well.[16] Edwin Black, similarly, implied that the use of the cancer metaphor for describing communism in the 1950s might have biased our foreign policy by creating images of unrelenting, unthinking evil while hiding the basic humanity of those involved in communist movements.[17] Finally, Daniel Clendenin, from the Graduate School at Drew University, looked at a series of pamphlets published between 1835 and 1908. Each pamphlet concerned the relation between science and religion, and every pamphlet used a war metaphor to describe that relation. While Clendenin did not speculate about the possible implications of the metaphor, he did note that over half of the pamphlets attacked the metaphor as being untrue and potentially dangerous.[18]

While we cannot be sure that these authors are all reaching valid conclusions, they are all well-respected in their fields, and their work seems cautious and scholarly. If we can, indeed, place some faith in their collective conclusion that the use of metaphor in public discourse can shape, as well as reflect, reality, then the Moral Majority's use of the war metaphor could have a great deal of significance and a criticism of that metaphor could reveal a lot about the movement.

A summary of our review of writings about metaphor substantiates three arguments. First, metaphor is a powerful trope, since a good metaphor can involve an audience in the discourse by forcing them to participate in deciphering its significance. Second, a good metaphor is energetic, and inapt or excessive use can kill a metaphor. While it is hard to tell whether a metaphor is alive or dead, Booth's *topoi* offer a framework within which to begin analysis. Finally, metaphors may serve to "focus on one aspect of reality [and] . . . keep us from focusing on other aspects of the concept that are inconsistent with that metaphor."[19] Our next task, then, is to describe and understand the Moral Majority's use of metaphor.

THE MORAL MAJORITY'S WAR

The Moral Majority, from its inception, pursued a war on the liberal and secular elements of American society. This war was waged with varying degrees of intensity and against various opponents. There were times at which the war seemed more distant, and there were opponents against whom no war was declared. Notwithstanding these bits of neutrality, the war metaphor stood out among the Moral Majority's array of rhetorical weapons: no alternative metaphor was pursued for as long nor in as many different ways, and none became as fully worked out as the war metaphor.

In this section, we will approach the war metaphor in several distinct ways. First, we will look at an extended example of the use of war imagery as a way of getting a better sense for the context of the war imagery. Second, we will examine the war in greater detail by using two topical systems: Ronald Reid's delineation of pro-war *topoi* and Booth's *topoi* for determining effective metaphors.

We can use a 1981 article by Moral Majority Vice-President Cal Thomas as the source for some war imagery.[20] The subject of the article was the criticism that the Reverend Falwell and those sympathetic to his views had received in the preceding year. The relevant portions of that article include:

[paragraph 2] Make no mistake about it, the battle over moral issues is intensifying throughout the nation. Critics of the conservative movement in general and the Moral Majority in particular are on the offensive as never before. . . .

[paragraph 3] Truth has been a major casualty of this all-out attack.

[paragraph 5] Even those who are not members of Moral Majority are facing unprecedented attacks simply for holding to a philosophy that is unpopular with liberals.

[paragraph 6] This is the reason why Dr. Falwell is so often referred to as a "Hitler" or an "Ayatollah." . . . [his critics] prefer to mount personal attacks.

[paragraph 9] Conservatives have been losing for years. They have almost learned how to be noble in defeat. But, conservatives never made a career out of blaming "evil" and "sinister" and "dangerous" forces for defeats.

[paragraph 18] "We do not intend to take the attacks lying down," Falwell said. "We do plan to counter-attack. Conservative Americans must not kid themselves. The battle isn't over with just one election. That was only the trumpet signalling the arrival of new troops. Every pro-moral American must be trained and motivated to fight over the long haul."

There were explicit war appeals in twelve of the article's twenty-two paragraphs. Eight of the remaining ten paragraphs argued that liberals in the media were attempting to destroy the Moral Majority by slandering it. If considered as a sort of "fifth column" effort, these references would also feed the war metaphor, but Thomas did not explicitly argue this.

This article clearly identified the presence of a war. It indicated that the enemy was pornographers, abortionists, liberal columnists, and others, and claimed that their aims were to destroy the Reverend Falwell's credibility and his movement. It indicated that "we" were pro-moral and conservative Americans, and that the stakes were apocalyptic: "we dare not give America back to the liberals who nearly destroyed it while it was theirs!" There was, however, no explicit weighing of the prospects for victory.

We may be able to make more sense out of the metaphor by analyzing it through two rhetorical models. The first of these is Ronald Reid's *topoi*, or themes, of pro-war rhetoric. Drawing upon Harold Laswell's study of World War I propaganda and primary sources from the French, Spanish, and Vietnamese wars, Reid concluded that: "[When] people are persuaded that (1) their territory, especially the center of their territory, is endangered, (2) the enemy is a barbarian who threatens their basic values, and (3) the prospects for victory are good, they display an amazing willingness to fight.[21] Reid found these appeals to be prevalent in the wars he examined. Robert Ivie found the same to be true in his examination of the War of 1812, although he used somewhat different labels for his *topoi*.[22]

Comparing Falwell's "war" rhetoric with that of rhetors in actual conflicts may help us to understand how seriously the Moral Majority took its war. If we find that the Moral Majority's rhetoric consistently used the same *topoi* as those found in real wars, then it is likely that Falwell's forces took their war seriously indeed. In such an instance, there was a greater risk that the metaphor functioned to shape the Moral Majority's view of reality—they may actually, on a day-to-day basis, have found apocalypses, fifth columns, cowardice under fire, appeasement, and a host of other threatening realities. If, contrarily, the metaphor was used only sporadically or in a pro forma fashion, then it was likely that the war was "dead." This would imply that war images were retained only as ornaments and that the Moral Majority confronted a reality that had been shaped by other forces.

We can begin by examining Reid's first *topus*, that of territoriality. The notion here was that people reacted most vigorously to incursions on their own land and that the intensity of their resistance grew as the invading forces moved toward the "heart" of their territory. A rhetor was better off when actual territory had been assaulted, as in Franklin Roosevelt's Pearl Harbor address, and considerably worse off when there was no actual imminent threat. American officials' difficulty in justifying the war in Vietnam to the manifestly unthreatened public might be witness to this observation. The territoriality theme implied a second important notion: that a war should be defensive. Since no one wants to cope with being cast in the role of aggressor, it is better to portray outraged innocence that is merely responding to the barbarity of the other side. Such appeals stress the notion that the other side started the conflict, and that our side was merely trying to redress the balance and recover what was rightfully ours.

The Moral Majority's rhetoric consistently reflected these themes. A single issue of the *Moral Majority Report* can provide us with a wealth of illustrations. The Moral Majority decried, for example, "further invasions of the limits of morality," which implied that liberals were guilty of aggression against America's moral borders. Next, the Moral Majority promised to "mount a full-scale counter-offensive to drive the devils out."Rabbi Alexander Schindler was accused of having "in fact, openly declared war on the New Right" and "critics [were] on the offensive as never before." The un-American nature of these attacks was made clear when they were described as "unprecedented attacks simply for holding to a philosophy that is unpopular." Each of these images was consistent with the notion that the moral majority of Americans had been occupying ground that was definable both geographically (America) and metaphysically (moral America), and that liberal forces chose to invade them with an alien ideology. The consistency of this appeal can be demonstrated by looking at the frequency with which the Moral Majority applied the terms "attack"and "defend" and their synonyms, such as "assault" and "batter" versus "protect" and "counterattack." In examining titles of stories in the *Report*,[23] we see that, while conservative forces did sometimes attack, it was more than three times more likely that liberals would be portrayed as the aggressors. The situation concerning defense was even more striking because there was no single instance in which liberals were portrayed as defending anything, while conservatives did so on seven occasions.

Reid noted, however, that incursion alone is an insufficient justification for war. A second necessary element of war rhetoric is an ethnocentric appeal; that is, an attempt to describe our enemies as generically horrible and vastly threatening. This comes down to three specific arguments: (1) our opponents are "sub-human hate objects," (2) their actions threaten our most basic values, and (3) we are paragons of civilization and virtue.

In many instances, the Moral Majority chose to collapse the first two categories into one appeal wherein it allowed us to draw value judgments about our opponents based upon the atrocities they had committed or were soon to commit. Liberals, for example, "nearly plunged this country into moral decadence," and television executives chose to "destroy their own principles and standards" in pursuit of greater profits. As a result, the Moral Majority found it correct to portray them as "the various media of amorality and immorality." The liberals, who were guilty of numerous but unspecified "diabolical criminal acts" had also established a system whereby "we are being programmed, subtly but steadily, to accept gross sin and immorality as normal." This same image of invidious deception was advanced by the claim that "many of those who have so successfully dragged America into the moral sewer are now wrapping themselves in the American flag."

These "perverted enemies of freedom" who were "destroying babies by the millions" were able to continue because of their manipulation of the media, through which they defined "truth [as] that which serves the advancement of their cause."[24]

These depictions, of course, stand in sharp contrast to the image of Falwell's own supporters. The simplest way of depicting moral America is to look back at the Moral Majority's choice of terms in the "What is the Moral Majority?" pamphlet, which was examined in Chapter 1. There we find that Moral Majoritarians were pro-life, pro-moral, antidrug, pro-equality, and pro-freedom.[25] The Moral Majority's image was further defined by their news stories in the *Report*. In one 1985 issue, for example, there was a front-page story that described the good-natured play between Moral Majority Vice-President Ron Godwin and a group of healthy Ethiopian refugee children. Godwin's presence was in conjunction with a ten-day "mercy mission" by Moral Majority representatives who were seeking first-hand knowledge on how best to combat the famine in Ethiopia. Also on the front page was a story about the Reverend Falwell's induction into the "Broadcasting Hall of Fame," as a reward for his "outstanding achievements and lasting contributions." In presenting the award, Ben Armstrong, executive director of the National Religious Broadcasters, praised Falwell's work in founding the Moral Majority and in religious broadcasting, and noted that Falwell "has consistently led in the battle for decency and liberty." Both articles featured pictures of the benignly smiling Moral Majoritarians and their admirers. The same theme was continued by a full-page announcement, on page three, of the formation of the Moral Majority's Child Protection Task Force. The ad, headlined by a picture of President Reagan and a quotation about the importance of protecting children, announced the Moral Majority's intention to free the thousands of children who were held as "the slaves of perverted molesters."[26]

The final requirement for an effective pro-war rhetoric is to maintain the impression, or illusion, that the war can be won; in short, to maintain optimism. No one can deny our perverse fascination with martyrdom, and we are even more strongly drawn to the dramatic images of military forces that were wiped out to the last man. These latter encounters often grow into powerfully evocative myths, which include the battles at Thermopylae, Masada, and the Alamo, as well as the Polish ghetto and Hungarian uprisings. Nonetheless, few people are enthusiastic about being drafted when they know in advance that defeat and disgrace await. The glory of such undertakings is ex post facto and, therefore, posthumous. The effective rhetor, then, must convince the audience that victory is possible and that things are going well.

The Moral Majority was extremely adept at this. In the early years, optimism was maintained through the theme "if God is on our side, who can stand against us?" With the disappearance of God in about 1981, the Moral Majority resorted to other techniques to maintain the aura of success. In part, they stressed positive themes in the *Report* articles. In the March 1985 issue, for example, we can find ten stories implying victory against only two setbacks. These victories included: the increasing health of Ethiopian children, Falwell's recognition by the "Hall of Fame," some medical advances on AIDS, the increasing strength of pro-prayer forces, the fact that Senate Majority Leader Bob Dole scheduled regular meetings with representatives of the "Conservative Movement," new federal regulations protecting the lives of premature and deformed infants, glee at the reorganization of the White House staff to better reflect conservative concerns, a federal appeals court ruling contrary to gay rights, favorable media coverage of the Moral Majority's Child Protection Task Force, and note of a legal appeal filed to reinstate Louisiana's creation-science law.[27] All of these reflected gains in areas the Moral Majority had previously defined as "battlefields." A survey of key words in *Report* article titles supported this view; conservatives were three times more likely to have victories than liberals, and the term "defeat", and its synonyms, were applied exclusively to liberal efforts.[28]

We can see, then, that Falwell's metaphor closely parallels the rhetoric of war. Any conclusions we attempt to draw from this need to be tempered, however, by the recollection that not all of the *Report* articles make use of the war metaphor. Overall, about 15-20 percent of the *Report* titles contain war images, although a number of articles without "war titles" contain war imagery in the text. Hence, while war is the most prevalent metaphor in the Moral Majority's rhetoric, it is not the only one, and the presence of the few competing metaphors may signal a greater degree of flexibility than one would find in an organization devoted solely to war imagery.

The second model is a synopsis of the characteristics of an effective metaphor. It was proposed by Wayne Booth, who, as we have noted, claimed that its components are implicit in any handbook of rhetorical theory from Aristotle to Whately. Booth used five standards to evaluate metaphors. He claimed that

good metaphors need to be active, concise, appropriate, accommodated, and ethos-building.

At the outset, we should note that there are several difficulties
in using Professor Booth's list. First, the process of assessing
metaphors remains highly subjective. While Booth did direct us
to a series of commonplaces, he did not tell us how to decide
whether the metaphor met the standard. For example, Booth
claimed that the metaphor should be appropriate to the
seriousness of the subject. It is, however, difficult to say how
serious each subject is. The outcomes of the American political
process may influence the fate of billions of lives, and yet we
persistently describe it in terms of a "game" metaphor.
Arguably, there is a great schism between the seriousness of the
subject and the metaphor, but the metaphor thrives. Similarly,
the course of the American economy is described in terms of a
"travel" metaphor, as when we speak of "a rocky road ahead"
or "a long way to go." We cannot be sure, however, how
serious the travel metaphor is, since the mere act of traveling
does not seem to imply either a particularly trivial decision or a
momentous one. Then again, Falwell declared "war" on
publisher Larry Flynt for Flynt's satiric suggestion that Falwell
had engaged in an incestuous relationship with his mother, a
particularly dour woman. The legal status of Flynt's action is
unclear, since a jury ruled that the statement was not libelous,
but nonetheless awarded damages to the Reverend Falwell. Regardless of its legal status, it is unclear that this affront is severe
enough to warrant combat.

Second, there is no clear way of resolving conflicting findings.
That is, there is no rule for interpreting a metaphor that meets
four of the standards, but not a fifth. We can, certainly, say that
this indicates that the metaphor is not as effective as it could be,
but this judgment seems a bit vacuous. As a result, we are
probably better off viewing this list as a heuristic device, a tool
for provoking thought rather than as a definitive judgment.

Booth's first claim is that metaphors should be active; that is,
they should "lend the energy of animated things to whatever
is less energetic or more abstract."[29] This is one of the prime
functions of metaphor. There is good reason to believe that the
war metaphor is particularly apt in this regard, since war is

perceived as a dynamic force for unifying, idealizing, and directing whole communities. Philosopher William James expressed the popular view of a war-free society:

[War's] "horrors" are a cheap price to pay for rescue from the only alternative supposed, of a world of clerk and teachers, of co-education and zoophily, of "consumer's leagues" and "associated charities," of industrialism unlimited and feminism unabashed. No scorn, no hardness, no valour any more! Fie upon such a cattleyard of a planet![30]

The point here is clear: war was considered too important to surrender, which led James to propose his notion of a "moral equivalence of war" as a less violent way of calling forth the same virtues in a "war" against the forces of nature. Robert Ivie, more recently, made about the same point: "No trope is inherently more understandable nor seemingly more realistic during times of crisis than that of force. When embellished by the art of rhetoric into a full-blown image of savagery, it transcends all definitions of reality and elevates every issue to a desperate struggle for survival."[31] We can conclude the war has the potential for producing an active metaphor.

Booth's second claim was that the metaphor should be concise. The general rule seemed to be "the more you convey in a given number of words, the better."[32] This implied that we were not looking just for the smallest number of words to use, but rather those words and images that triggered the greatest response in the audience. Again, war seems workable because the subject is so widely explored in American popular culture. Television and motion pictures glorify America's past wars and the fact that many of our heroes (from Ethan Allen to Eisenhower) were military leaders. As a result, we can all bring an enormous array of associations to the Moral Majority's various war messages. We can take, for example, the statement, "the battle isn't over with just one election. That was only the trumpet signaling the arrival of new troops."[33] This passage calls to mind the Indian Wars, which were the heyday of the cavalry trumpeters. We can see a small, but gallant, circle of troopers running low on ammunition. John Wayne is either in the circle or commanding the relief column. Our troopers are surrounded by a barbaric horde of Indians: stealthy savages trying to wrest control of the land from peaceful settlers by committing atrocities. Both the judgment of history and the conventions of film-making tell us that the relief detachment will prove adequate to kill a satisfying number of these barely human creatures. The remnant will withdraw into the hills and bide its time until our guard is down. Then some hot-eyed brave will lead them into another bloody foray.

We do not need to accept this vision word for word. It should suffice to agree on the general script; after that we can supply our own details. Regardless of whether the locale is Concord, the Alamo, or Bastogne, the images of fiendish barbarism, desperate gallantry, and ultimate victory are all available.

The third criterion is that the metaphor should be appropriate to the subject depicted. We have already discussed some of the difficulties in assessing whether or not this criterion has been met. Given its tendency toward the apocalyptic, the war metaphor seems both natural and appropriate for the Moral Majority's crusade.

The fourth criterion is that the metaphor should be accommodated to its audience. This means the hearers should have some special affinity for or identification with the metaphor. Although there were a number of ways of construing Falwell's likely audience, the metaphor was probably accommodated to any of them. For the sake of simplicity, we can reduce the Moral Majority's probable audiences down to two: we may either assume that the Moral Majority was writing for a general cross-section of the American populace or for the fundamentalist subset who were the Reverend Falwell's religious following.

There were a number of reasons for believing that the general population might identify with the war metaphor. First, we can note that a great deal of intellectual energy had been devoted to analyzing the causes, strategies, and effects of war; for example, a thousand books on war were published in English between 1946 and 1966. Worldwide, we know of at least 1,300 bibliographies on war, 20 bibliographies of bibliographies on war, and one bibliography of bibliographies of bibliographies on war.[34] In a related vein, a survey of the titles of books published in the last eighty years shows frequent use of the war metaphor. We have, according to these titles, declared wars on: cancer, disease, the saints, gold, hunger, the image of God in man, the poor, poverty, privacy, the bank of the United States, the mind, want, and world poverty. Indeed, we had even declared war on war.[35] Both of these surveys indicate a continued high level of interest in the study of war and war metaphors.

We can also find proof that the war metaphor has entered the public consciousness. For example, by examining titles and subtitles of *Time* and *Newsweek* articles for the first six months of 1983, we find that war represented the single most common metaphor for describing our social and political life. *Newsweek* used three dozen war metaphors and fewer than two dozen game metaphors, which constituted the next most popular category. The significance of the war metaphor was highlighted by its ability to be applied to a wide variety of situations, whereas the game metaphor applied almost exclusively to a single setting, electoral politics. Thus, game metaphors were largely limited to claims such as "Campaign Teams Shaping Up" and "Real Horse Race of '84," while war metaphors ranged from "Onward Consumer Soldiers," "New War on Health Costs," and "Indian Water Wars" to "Reagan . . . Under Attack," "Reagan on the Defense," "Reagan Sounds the Alarm," and "[Reagan's] Unspoken Defense."[36]

Of somewhat greater significance were the extended "wars" that have been periodically declared by America's presidents. The significance of these acts derived from the fact that these appeared to represent conscious, ongoing efforts to capitalize on the power of war images. Over the last two decades, every president has declared at least one major domestic war. President Johnson declared war on poverty. President Nixon declared war on cancer. President Ford declared war on inflation. President Carter declared war on energy-import dependence. President Reagan declared war on drug smuggling, and President Bush declared war on drugs.[37] We may take President Reagan's October 1982 address declaring war on drug smuggling as representative of these speeches:

I have good news for you—a major initiative that I believe can mark a turning point in the battle against crime . . . we will establish task forces in key areas . . . to mount an intensive and coordinated campaign . . . [and] this administration will open a new legislative offensive . . . I believe this program will prove to be a highly effective attack on drug trafficking . . . [which represents] an invisible empire in our midst.[38]

This quotation highlights the fact that Mr. Reagan did not declare this war lightly or as an afterthought. Rather, it appears to be an integral part of the way in which we were supposed to perceive these social realities and to comprehend appropriate responses to them.

The general American population should, then, be fairly comfortable with the use of a war metaphor to frame social action. Over the years, their scholars and presidents have used the metaphor and the mass media have popularized it. This does not imply that most people would react sanguinely to Falwell's use of the metaphor, since the war language might just serve to reinforce their image of him as an American Hitler or Ayatollah, but they would find the metaphor comprehensible.

The fundamentalist subset of the population should be even more amenable to the metaphor. We should, first, remember that all of the reasons that apply to the general population also apply to the fundamentalists. There are two additional reasons for assuming the fundamentalists would be comfortable with the war metaphor. First, there are a number of elements of the Christian religion that rely heavily on the war metaphor. For example, the two most common metaphors for describing the proper role of a Christian are the soldier and the slave. These metaphors are reinforced by many hymns that rely on war imagery. Depending upon the hymnal consulted, between 5 and 18 percent of all hymns depend on a war motif. Among the more common hymns would be "The Battle Hymn of the Republic," "Onward, Christian Soldiers," "A Mighty Fortress," and "Lord God of Hosts."[39] Thus, we should expect that people who made a considerable investment in their religion should have been familiar with these images and would have found their use natural.

The unique culture of fundamentalism provided a second

reason why the war metaphor was well-matched to its audience. In a nutshell, Falwell's people lived in a state of constant siege, and this condition should have heightened their receptivity to the war rhetoric. This siege mentality drew from numerous sources. Falwell's theology taught that Christ was a rather "macho" character, as opposed to the frail figure that often depicts Him. These views were also reflected in the sermons of Billy Sunday, who portrayed Christ as someone capable of punching people in the nose.[40] This pugnacity seemed to be necessary given the fundamentalists' premillennial philosophy, which preached that Christ will twice be called upon to lead an army of saints against the forces of the anti-Christ, once at Armageddon and again after a thousand-year reign. This theology helped explain why the fundamentalists strove for separation from the sinful world over the past sixty or seventy years. This separation helped reinforce the war mentality by setting the fundamentalists at odds with the surrounding society. They were, for example, vilified for their refusal to fight in World War I; in reaction, many combined increased militancy with withdrawal from society.[41] Having withdrawn, they came to expect attacks from the unsaved about them. The Reverend Carl McIntire, an exponent of Falwell's brand of fundamentalism, wrote that "separation involves hard, gruelling controversy. It involves attacks, personal attacks, even violent attacks." His conclusion was that aggression could be "an expression of Christian love."[42] Falwell explained the result when he wrote that "fundamentalists like me were taught to fight before we were taught to read and write."[43] Therefore, the fundamentalists' generally high level of involvement with religion in general and with fundamentalism in particular should have made the war metaphor uniquely well-suited to their needs.

Booth's final criterion for an effective metaphor was that it helped build the ethos of the speaker. The task here is to build or sustain the speaker's image as one worthy of trust. This accomplishment seems implicit in the war metaphor, since our leader in wartime is a person to whom we entrust our lives, property, and sacred honor. He or she is a person to whom we give life-or-death powers. Implicitly, then, Falwell was cast into the role of an utterly responsible Supreme Commander.

We can, then, advance two conclusions about the Moral Majority's war. First, our comparison of the rhetoric of this metaphorical war with actual conflicts suggests that the Moral Majority took its war seriously. This conclusion is buttressed by our findings that the war is developed across a variety of issues, that it provides an overarching structure to many of the messages, and that the types of appeals raised by Falwell closely paralleled those used by rhetors in prosecuting real wars. Second, our application of Professor Booth's criteria imply that the war metaphor should have been an effective device for mobilizing support on a variety of issues.

THE DECLINE OF THE WAR METAPHOR

Our findings concerning changes in the war metaphor can be summarized simply: the war nearly disappeared from the pages of the *Moral Majority Report* by 1985. In this section, we will briefly note the extent of this change and then look at its causes.

A simple content analysis of the *Report* allows us to establish the frequency of the war metaphor. Using the same sample of the *Report* upon which we had previously relied, we find a distinct pattern of change in the prevalence of the war metaphor. In 1980, 10.3 percent of all articles contained war imagery in the title, subtitle, internal headings, block quotations, first paragraph, or last paragraph.[44] In 1981, this grew to 21.2 percent, and the frequency peaked in 1982 at 25.4 percent. A steady decline followed: 19.6 percent in 1983, 8.9 percent in 1984, and 4.9 percent in 1985.

We can further break down these changes by looking at changes by type of issue. For the sake of clarity, all of the articles in our sample can be placed into one of the eight major categories discussed earlier: Government and Politics, National Security, Inside Moral Majority, Education, Morality, Economics, Human Life, and The Rest of the News.[45] To clarify the comparisons, we can look at two-year cycles: 1980-81, 1982-83, and 1984-85. Each two-year group contained one national election year and one nonelection year, which helped to control for the possibility that election years are more bellicose than others.

Some of the categories never used war metaphors. Inside Moral Majority, Economics, and The Rest of the News had one war metaphor between them over six years. Some categories showed no consistent change over time. National Security and Human Life showed somewhat higher incidences of war imagery in the middle period than either the beginning or the end; this is consistent with our total sample. Some categories showed minor, but distinct, declines in the metaphor; Education and Morality are examples. The greatest change occurred in the Government and Politics category. There was a precipitous decline in the war metaphor over the last two years: after registering eleven war metaphors in each of the first two periods, which is about as many as all the other categories combined, there was only one war metaphor in the last two years. This represented a 91 percent decline between 1984-85 and either of the earlier periods.

We can plausibly attribute changes in the *Report*'s use of the metaphor to two factors. The first factor was the increasing professionalism of the *Report*. As we have noted earlier, the *Report* went through a long series of changes designed to increase its ethos and reputation as a legitimate forum. It seems likely that the more journalistic style that dominated in the final years militated against the fervent rhetoric implied by the war metaphor. This may also help to explain why there were no new metaphors introduced to replace war. There had been a few, halting efforts to invoke an "awakening" metaphor, but months passed between one invocation and the next. Instead, much of the *Report*'s language is largely literal. This is consistent with the straightforward style affected by journalists.

A second reason for the shift in the *Report*'s style was that Falwell gained a new political legitimacy that made a war on the system unnecessary. We know, for example, that Falwell felt sufficiently secure to hold frequent public encounters with Senator Edward Kennedy, the Senate's most liberal member, and even to boast that he and Senator Kennedy frequently prayed and fellowshipped together.[46] Similarly, both Falwell and Vice-President Godwin stressed in late interviews that they now considered themselves to be "insiders."[47] Even the astonishing decline in press coverage of Falwell and the Moral Majority spoke to their legitimacy: Falwell was so much a part of the political scene that his declarations and policy gains were no longer seen as newsworthy.[48]

Our summary can be brief. We looked at metaphor because it is a powerful trope and, presumably, a good indicator of a rhetor's style. We found that the Moral Majority had seriously but unimaginatively advanced a war metaphor as the prime device by which it organized its communications. The metaphor's progressive decline implies that the Moral Majority viewed the world less hostilely as time progressed. This is consistent with our more extended case studies in Chapter 4 and confirms the notion that the Moral Majority sought to pursue its vision with less rigidity and less animosity as the organization aged.

NOTES

1. "Rev. Falwell Meets an Outspoken Antagonist, Yale's Giamatti," *New York Times*, 12 November 1982, p. B4.

2. Frances Fitzgerald, "A Disciplined, Charging Army," *The New Yorker*, 18 May 1981, p. 110.

3. Aristotle, *Rhetoric*, 3. 10. 1410 b .17; Kenneth Burke, *A Grammar of Motives* (Princeton, N.J., Prentice-Hall, 1945; University of California Press paperback edition, 1969), p. 503.

4. Aristotle, *Rhetoric*, 3. 2. 1405b4. This is a fairly common way of viewing metaphors. Ted Cohen, for example, spent considerable time explaining our need to "declipher" the "joke" implied by a good metaphor. Ted Cohen, "Metaphor and the Cultivation of Intimacy," in *On Metaphor*, Sheldon Sacks, ed. (Chicago: University of Chicago Press, 1979), pp. 7-8.

5. This is an adaptation of Osborne and Ehninger's treatment of metaphor. Michael Osborne and Douglas Ehninger, "The Metaphor in Public Address," *Speech Monographs*, 29 (1962): 223-34, cited by Jane Blankenship and Barbara Sweeney, "The 'Energy' of Form," *Central States Speech Journal*, 31 (1980): 179.

6. Aristotle, *Rhetoric*, 3. 10. 1410b10, quoted in *The Social Use of Metaphor*, David Sapir and Christopher Crocker, eds. (Philadelphia: University of Pennsylvania Press, 1977), unnumbered page after "Preface." Sapir and Crocker do not indicate the translator's identity.

7. Hermann Stelzner, "Analysis by Metaphor," *Quarterly Journal of Speech*, 51 (February 1965): 60; Philip Wheelwright, *The Burning*

Fountain: A Study in the Language of Symbolism (Bloomington: University of Indiana Press, 1968), p. 102; Martin Foss, quoted in *The Burning Fountain*, p. 104; Earl MacCormac, "Religious Metaphors: Mediators Between Biological and Cultural Evolution That Generate Transcendent Meaning," *Zygon*, 19 (March 1983): 55; Blankenship and Sweeney, "'Energy' of Form," p. 179.

8. Herb Simons, "Some Questions About *Metaphors We Live By*," Seminar of *Metaphors We Live By*, 26 January 1981; MacCormac, "Religious Metaphors," p. 55.

9. Edwin Black, *Rhetorical Criticism: A Study in Method* (New York: MacMillan, 1965; University of Wisconsin paperback edition, 1978).

10. Wayne Booth, "Metaphor as Rhetoric: The Problem of Evaluation," in *On Metaphor*, pp. 54-5. Booth made a distinction between "weapon metaphors," which were intended to be perceived, and "sublime metaphors," which were the pervasive, underlying metaphors around which an entire society might function. Booth's use of the term "weapon metaphor" is unrelated to our subsequent references to "war" and "military" metphors.

11. Some discussion of the different metaphors that may explain brain function may be found in: Elizabeth Loftus, *Eyewitness Testimony* (Cambridge, MA: Harvard University Press, 1979); Richard Restak, *The Brain: The Last Frontier* (New York: Warner Books paperback edition, 1979), pp. 185-186, 233-236; and Ulric Neisser, "The Processes of Vision," *Scientific American*, 219 (September 1968): 204-214.

12. George Lakoff and Mark Johson, *Metaphors We Live By* (Chicago: University of Chicago Press, 1980), p. 10.

13. William Leuchtenberg, "The New Deal and the Analogue of War," in *Change and Continuity in Twentiety-Century America*, John Braeman, Robert Bremner, and Everett Walter, eds. (Columbus, OH: Ohio State University Press, 1964), pp. 81-143.

14. Stelzner, "Analysis," pp. 59-61; Lakoff and Johnson, *Metaphors*, pp. 4-7.

15. Lakoff and Johnson, *Metaphors*, pp. 7, 4.

16. William Leogrande, "Salvador's No Domino," *New York Times*, 9 March 1983, p. A23.

17. Edwin Black, "The Second Persona," *Quarterly Journal of Speech*, 56 (April 1970): 109-119.

18. Daniel Clendenin, "Exploring the Military Metaphor: Science and Religion in the 19th Century," *Drew Gateway*, Summer 1973, p. 10.

19. Lakoff and Johnson, *Metaphors*, p. 10.

20. Cal Thomas, "Liberals Launch Vicious Attacks on 'New Right,'" *Moral Majority Report*, 16 March 1981, pp. 12-13. Hereafter, this publication will be abbreviated as *Report*.

21. Ronald Reid, "New England Rhetoric and the French War, 1675-1769: A Case Study in the Rhetoric of War," *Communication Monographs*, 43 (November 1976): 284.

22. Robert Ivie, "The Metaphor of Force in Prowar Discourse: The Case of 1812," *Quarterly Journal of Speech*, 68 (August 1982): 240-253. Ivie pursues the same themes in two other articles: "Presidential Motives for War," *Quarterly Journal of Speech*, 60 (October 1974): 337-345, and "Image of Savagery in American Justifications for War," *Communication Monographs*, 47 (1980): 279-294.

23. This is based on an examination of all titles in a sample of *Report* from 1980 to 1985. The March, June, and September issues were examined.

24. *Report*, 16 March 1981, pp. 6, 7, 8, 9, 15; *Report*, 14 March 1980, p. 16.

25. Jerry Falwell, "What Is the Moral Majority?" pamphlet, 1983, n.p.

26. *Report*, March 1985, pp. 1-3.

27. *Report*, March 1985, pp. 1-21.

28. This is part of the same examination discused in note 25.

29. Booth, "Metaphor as Rhetoric," p. 54.

30. Margaret Knight, ed., *William James* (London: Pelican Books, 1950), p. 242.

31. Ivie, "The Metaphor of Force," p. 253.

32. Booth, "Metaphors as Rhetoric," p. 55.

33. Jerry Falwell, quoted in Thomas, "Liberals Launch," p. 13.

34. Alastair Buchanan, *War in Modern Society* (New York: Harper & Row, 1966), p. 199; *Peace and War: A Guide to Bibliographies*, Berenice Carroll, ed. (Santa Barbara, CA: ABC-Clio, 1983).

35. Edward Podolsky, *The War on Cancer* (New York: Reinhold, 1943); Harriette Chick, *War on Disease* (London: A. Deutsch, 1971); Jesse Penn-Lewis, *War on the Saints* (Ft. Washington, PA: Christian Literature Crusade, revised ed., 1964); Anthony Sutton, *War on Gold*, (Seattle, WA: Self-Counsel Press, 1979); Agency for International Development, *War on Hunger* (Washington, DC: AID, 1977); Margaret Stucki, *War on Light; The Destruction of the Image of God in Man Through Modern Art* (Rogers, AR: Bird's Meadow Publishing, 1975); Clarence Carson, *War on the Poor* (New Rochelle, NY: Arlington House, 1969); Hubert Humphrey, *War on Poverty* (New York: McGraw-Hill, 1964); Frank Alexander, *War on Poverty: Twenty-Four Skirmishes* (Ithaca, NY: Cornell University Press, 1970); *War on Proverty*, Louis Lander, ed. (New York: Facts on File, 1967); Reuben Margolin, *War on Poverty*, (W. Haven, CT: Pendulum Press, 1969); *War on Privacy*, Lester Sobel, ed. (New York: Facts on File, 1976); Thomas Gordon, *War on the Bank of the United States* (New York: A.M. Kelley, 1968, reprint of 1834 ed.); Peter Watson, *War*

on the Mind (New York; Basic Books, 1978); Conference on the U.N. Development Decade, *War on Want* (New York: United Nations, 1962); Harold Wilson, *War on World Poverty* (Millwood, NY: Krause Reprints, 1969, reprint of 1953 ed.); Frederick Libby, *War on War* (Washington, D.C.: National Council for Reductions in Armaments, 1922).

36. All citations are from *Newsweek* in 1983: "Campaign Teams Shaping Up," 4 April, p. 15; "Real Horse Race for '84," 27 June, p. 22; "Reagan at Midterm: His Policies Under Attack," 31 January, p. 24; "Reagan Sounds the Alarm," 14 March, p. 16; "Reagan on the Defense," 18 April, p. 22; "Onward Consumer Soldiers," 25 April, p. 56; "New War on Health Care Costs," 9 May, p. 24; and "Indian Water Wars," 13 June, p. 80.

37. U.S., President, *Public Papers of the Presidents of the United States* (Washington, D.C.: Office of the Federal Register, National Archives and Records Service), Lyndon B. Johnson, 1964, pp. 375-380; Richard M. Nixon, 1971, pp. 1205-1206; Gerald R. Ford, 1974, pp. 205-210; James E. Carter, 1977, pp. 656-662; and, Ronald W. Reagan, 1982, pp. 1313-1317. George Bush, "Address to the Nation on the National Drug Control Stragegy," *Weekly Compilation of Presidential Documents*, Week ending September 11, 1989, pp. 1304-1308.

38. *Public Papers*, Reagan, pp. 1313, 1316.

39. For examples of such hymns, see: Albert Christ-James, ed., *American Hymns Old and New* (New York: Columbia University Press, 1980), especially "Hymns of War and Peace," pp. 281-292, and "Baptist Hymns," pp. 417-439; *Hymns of the Christian Life* (Harrisburg, PA: Christian Publications, 1962); and E.E. Ryden, *The Story of Christian Hymnody* (Rock Island, IL: Augustana Press, 1959), especially "Hymns of Crusading Spirits," pp. 567-571. Sandra Sizer, *Gospel Hymns and Social Religion: The Rhetoric of Nineteenth Century Revivalism* (Philadelphia: Temple University Press, 1978) makes three particularly useful comments. First, just looking at the number of battle hymns underestimates their significance because this category contains some of the world's most popular hymns (p. 40). Second, Christian hymns almost always stress the defensive nature of their conflict (p. 41). Third, between 5 percent and 12 percent of all hymns contain a war metaphor (p. 171, Table 2).

40. Fitzgerald, "Changing Army," pp. 109-110.

41. Fitzgerald, "Changing Army," pp. 111-112; David Harrel, "The Roots of the Moral Majority: Fundamentalism Revisited," *Occasional Papers* (Collegeville, MN: Institute for Ecumenical and Cultural Research, 1981), pp. 7-9.

42. Carl T. McIntire, quoted by Fitzgerald, "Changing Army," p. 109.

43. Jerry Falwell, "An Interview with the Lone Ranger of American Fundamentalism," *Christianity Today*, 4 September 1981, p. 23.

44. These indicators were chosen for two reasons: first, they represented highlights of the article, so that we may assume that the metaphor would be manifested in, at least, one of them if it were in the article. Second, they made it possible to survey large numbers of articles in a relatively short time, which allowed a corresponding increase in the size of the sample.

45. These represent the main internal categories in the *Report* since its last revision. In order to extend this categorization to earlier issues, I listed all of the articles that have appeared under each category and then used that term as a way of determining which articles in each earlier issue would have fallen into each category.

46. "Kennedy Charms the Evangelists, but Falwell Still Outshines Him," *San Francisco Examiner*, 6 February 1985; "The Ted and Jerry Show," *San Francisco Chronicle*, 3 February 1985.

47. "Religious Right Feel the Pull of Pluralism," *Washington Post*, 27 December 1984, pp. 1, 12.

48. A computerized search of the *National Magazine Index*, for example, showed one article under "Moral Majority" in 1979, 27 in 1980, 100 in 1981, 37 in 1982, 14 in 1983, 6 in 1984, and 4 in 1985. A similar search of the *National Newspaper Index* showed 17 articles for 1980, 68 for 1981, 18 for 1982, 16 for 1983, 25 for 1984, and 6 for 1985.

Chapter 6

"Our Mission Has Been Accomplished"

This is your final letter from M.M. . . . please read every word carefully.
> Jerry Falwell, 6 January 1986[1]

We haven't seen the last of Jerry Falwell.
> Mary Hanna, Columnist, 22 June 1989[2]

At 10:00 A.M., January 6, 1986, the Moral Majority slipped into a quiet grave. At that moment, the Reverend Falwell announced to the National Press Club in Washington, D C the formation of a new group, the Liberty Federation, which would completely subsume the Moral Majority. While the Reverend Falwell adamantly argued that the Moral Majority was not "going out of business," the facts contradicted him. The Moral Majority had virtually vanished from the public eye, fund-raising was in a tailspin, lobbying had virtually halted, and Falwell had taken to directing large chunks of income out of the Moral Majority accounts and into those of his church.[3] Falwell argued that the Moral Majority would continue to function as a subset of the Liberty Federation, but there was little substance behind the claim. In analyzing the demise of the Moral Majority, Jeffrey K. Hadden, a sociologist with the University of Virginia and co-author of *Prime-Time Preachers*, claimed that, "Moral Majority has not had the sustained, organizational grassroots thrust [Falwell] now wishes it had. It functions primarily as a mail organization."[4] Falwell, in creating the Liberty Federation, stripped the Moral Majority of its access to the mails. He wrote in his January 6 letter that, "this is the last time I will write to you on behalf of the Moral Majority."[5] At the same time, he changed the *Moral Majority Report* to the *Liberty Report*. If the Moral Majority existed only through its communications and those communications were permanently ended, then the organization itself had come to its end.

Falwell tried to maintain a semblance of political organization for several more years. The Liberty Federation limped along for three years, garnering virtually no media coverage and raising even less money.[6] Falwell resigned the organization's presidency in November of 1987, announced his withdrawal from political life in 1988, and finally put an end to the whole operation in June of 1989. Finding the best explanation for a bad situation, Falwell proclaimed victory: "The purpose of the Moral Majority was to activate the religious right. Our mission has been accomplished."[7] The organization had fallen so low that the one-sentence story of its passing in *USA Today* was thirteenth in a fourteen-story column, after announcements of a new "quiet time" rule for county treasury workers in Tacoma and of a seminar for female professional pilots. Humorist Mark Russell reflected the general reaction to Falwell's claim of victory: "Falwell says all their goals were accomplished. Abortion is illegal, prayer is back in the schools, Pat Robertson is President and Tammy Bakker is Queen of the May."[8]

Having seen the Moral Majority from its birth through its death by way of a tumultuous and unpopular life, some reflections seem in order. We should first review what we have learned about the changing rhetoric of the Moral Majority. Second, we should look at what killed the Moral Majority. Finally, we should attempt some judgment on the work of the Moral Majority, and specifically, on how we might assess the success of the organization and its rhetoric.

A SUMMARY REVIEW

Our conclusions about the changing rhetoric of the Moral Majority can be stated simply: the organization's strongly moralistic rhetoric evolved over time to reflect less strident tones and greater political awareness, while the subjects of that rhetoric (such as abortion, school prayer, and homosexuality) changed little. Although these changes seemed little appreciated, much less emulated, by political and academic critics of the Moral Majority, their presence had been observed and predicted by a number of thoughtful writers. By late 1984, neo-conservative sociologist and columnist Michael Novak wrote that "by entering the national debate, [the Moral Majority] have been obliged to rethink their positions, develop larger sensibilities, expand their horizons, learn new forms of cooperation and civil argument."[9]

We have made several specific findings concerning these changes. The first finding is that the Moral Majority had a relatively stable agenda across time. The issues that dominated the earlier agenda, such as abortion and church-state relations, continued as major concerns in the organization's last year. The changes that did occur were unsurprising. One change was the decline of mobilization and legitimation rhetoric after 1981; we have noted that this decline seemed directly linked to the success of that rhetoric. A second change was the rise of national security and international affairs as a central concern. These issues were stressed even in Falwell's *Listen, America!*[10] book and became quantitatively important by 1982. Finally, a series of changes occurred that represented the simple evolution of core issues; for example, AIDS became a major focus of the Moral Majority's gay rights debate after the magnitude of that disease became known.

Our second finding was that some changes occurred within the organization's treatment of individual issues. The most notable example of this "softening" was the shift on abortion to grant the acceptability of permitting some kinds of abortions to continue and to focus more attention on dealing with the causes of abortion. Such changes did not signal a change in the organization's desire to cope with these issues; rather they indicated strategic changes designed to produce better results.

Finally, we found fairly major shifts in the tone of the organization's rhetoric across time. In particular, its early rhetoric stressed the notion of uniquely "Christian" political action as an end and harshly militant rhetoric, epitomized by the war metaphor, as a means. By its last year, the war metaphor had been muted, pluralism had been embraced, and even arch-liberal Ted Kennedy received occasional kindly references.

Opposition rhetoric showed few corresponding changes. This intransigence may be attributed to a variety of factors: continuing to pain the Moral Majority in devil terms best served the opponents' political ends, the changes may have been too small to seem more than cosmetic, or the critics might have been too set in their judgments to be concerned with the possibility that they were incorrect. In any case, critics continued to the end to describe the Moral Majority as "holier-than-thou," "extremist," and hypocritical.[11]

WHAT KILLED THE MORAL MAJORITY?

There was nothing unique about the Liberty Federation. It never established an identity that was, in any way, separate from that of its predecessor organization. The office space, staff, mailing lists, computers, newspaper, and executive officers of the Moral Majority were all transferred, intact, to the Liberty Federation. Except for changing the term "Moral Majority" to "Liberty" in the newspaper's logo and changing the organiza-tion's letterhead paper, the only appreciable difference was the creation of the Liberty Alliance, which Falwell described as an educational and lobbying arm of the Federation.[12]

What we still do not know is why the Federation was created. The official explanation was that the current interests of the Moral Majority went beyond the limits set in its original charter and those implied by its name. Falwell explained in his National Press Club statement:

In the course of the past seven years, we have found ourselves drawn into issues and conflicts which were not anticipated in 1979 . . . many persons have felt that the Moral Majority name and charter are not broad enough to cover many of these domestic and international issues. We have therefore spent months discussing this problem with our national and state leaders. The end result has been the formation of a new organization which we have named The Liberty Federation.[13]

Falwell went on to list the issues that the Federation planned to address in its January 23-24, 1986, National Summit, which was to be a convocation of 550 national and state Liberty Federation leaders.

In the general sessions and workshops at the Summit, we will major in several areas: the 1986 Senatorial races; the education, registration and mobilization of one million new voters during this year; the recruitment of new grassroots support of The Liberty Federation; education of the American public on the importance of SDI, a Balanced Budget Amendment, continued strong national defense, and support for the State of Israel; and informing all Americans on Soviet-Cuban expansion in Central and South America; and other areas involving the Reagan Agenda.[14]

We were, Falwell elsewhere concluded, "engaging the enemy on new ground."[15]

Our review of the Moral Majority's agenda over its six years of existence provides only limited support for Falwell's claim of covering new ground. All of the issues mentioned in Falwell's National Press Club statement had been covered in earlier years of the *Moral Majority Report*, and some, such as mobilization of the electorate and support of Israel, dated from the *Report*'s very first issue. Falwell might claim that, while these issues were addressed, they were either inappropriate to the Moral Majority or were discussed too little. Neither of these claims is particularly strong. While foreign policy issues were not the hallmark of the Moral Majority's agenda, they represented a constant thread throughout the organization's history and became a major element by the midpoint of its existence. Moreover, *Listen, America!* dealt extensively with the moral and religious bases for opposition to communism and support for a strong national defense.

Similarly, the claim that these important issues were addressed too little was problematic. First, the *Moral Majority Report* ran cover stories on the Strategic Defense Initiative, Soviet disinformation campaigns, Nicaraguan involvement in drug smuggling, the African famines, and other major foreign stories in 1985, which shows a high level of involvement. Moreover, when we compare the contents of the first three 1986 issues of the *Liberty Report* with the first three 1985 issues of the *Moral Majority Report*, we find virtually no difference in the proportion of space devoted to international and economic news, the Federation's forte, versus traditional moral issues, the Moral Majority's focus. Speaking roughly, we find that the *Moral Majority Report* devoted the equivalent of eight full pages, between the three issues, to international and economic news, and fifteen pages to moral issues. In comparison, the *Liberty Reports* provided only about six pages of international and economic news, as compared to eighteen pages of moral coverage. The clear implication is that, at most, the Liberty Federation placed no greater emphasis on these issues than did its predecessor and might have, if we assume a fair degree of accuracy for these page counts, devoted slightly less space to the issues that justified its existence.

This should not be interpreted to mean that the Liberty Federation's professed interest in these matters was a sham. Our long-term analysis of the Moral Majority's agenda showed that international and economic issues were minor matters for the greater part of the organization's history, that their coverage was episodic, and that the emergence of international news as front-page issues was comparatively recent. This does mean, however, that a change in the organization should not have been necessary if its only justification was to permit discussion of these issues.

An interpretation that might reconcile these two factors is possible. The rise of the Moral Majority's international interest was coincident with a decline in the health of the organization. It is entirely possible that the Moral Majority's directors either interpreted the decline as the result of the poor fit between the organization's professed purpose and its new interests, or they felt that the decline might best be reversed by an organizational shakeup.

There is considerable circumstantial evidence to suggest that the organization was panicked by its condition in 1985.[16] We noted that extent of the budget shortfalls earlier. Similar declines were registered by a number of conservative political action groups; the National Conservative Political Action Committee ended 1984 with a $4 million debt, the Richard A. Viguerie Company faced millions in unpaid bills, and a variety of organizations went bankrupt.[17] Falwell repeatedly recognized the problem, but frequently changed his public estimation of its importance. At one point, he merely noted that fund-raising "went soft" over the summer months, but at another point claimed that his controversial defense of South Africa cost the organization over $1 million in contributions.[18] Similarly, 1985's last two mass-mailed letters from the Moral Majority were remarkably hysterical in their claims:

We need a $1 million miracle in the next few days or Moral Majority simply will not survive intact. We are on the verge of our worst calamity in our six-year history. I must ask you to prayerfully consider a $15 miracle gift.[19]

Eleven days later, on Christmas eve, Falwell wrote:

1985 has been our most difficult year ever . . . right now, Moral Majority is literally on the verge of collapse . . . As you know, I was forced to cancel the December issue of *Moral Majority Report* newspaper. The January issue has been put on indefinite hold. Next will come cutbacks in staff.[20]

On March 31, 1986, Falwell was forced to fire over 200 employees from various parts of his empire in response to financial problems.[21] However, two weeks after his Christmas epistle and two months before the mass firing, Falwell vehemently denied that the Moral Majority had been in financial jeopardy or that the creation of the Liberty Federation was brought on by economic pressure.[22]

Moreover, 1985 also saw a number of top-level administrative changes. By late summer, the two top officers of the Moral Majority, Cal Thomas and Rod Godwin, and two key aides in the electronic church (Nelson Keener, publisher of Falwell's *Fundamentalist Journal,* and Bill Paul, Liberty University's chief of financial affairs) left the organization. There was no public reason given for any of the job changes.[23]

Falwell recognized, in part, these declines but chose to attribute them to factors beyond the organization's control. Falwell explained in February 1986 that:

most people in the New Right would tell you they are having difficulty raising funds. That is true for two reasons. First, so many more organizations are raising funds out of the same pool. Second, the perception of safety, which our success has created, hurts fund-raising. You don't do well in fund-raising unless you are in trouble.[24]

It is possible that Falwell made a decision to broaden his organization's focus as a way to be more competitive in the race for funds. A former editor of the *Moral Majority Report* conceded that national security issues were, by far, more profitable mailings than those it devoted to conventional moral issues.[25] Moreover, in conservative fund-raising, Viguerie saw this trend intensifying:

Issues like the balanced-budget amendment, aid to the freedom fighters in Nicaragua will be on the front burners in the coming year or two. Consequently, social issues will be generating less interest than these other issues. So it's kind of natural that Falwell, who already had an interest in some of these issues, would want an organization that could deal with them.[26]

In this case, the creation of the Liberty Federation resulted less from the inability of the Moral Majority to attend to profitable issues than from Falwell's interest in achieving the widest possible publicity for is attention to popular, profitable ones.

The switch, however, was unsuccessful. It may have been a disaster. The Moral Majority always argued that it occupied a unique position in the world of conservative activist organizations. The organization derived its unique position from its focus on moral issues, whereas many of its competitors rushed willy-nilly to address every conceivable sort of claim. This allowed the Moral Majority to claim that its intent was to reclaim a moral heritage that had been squandered during decades of liberal misrule. Falwell himself noted in 1981 that:

We grew because we touched a raw nerve in the American electorate. Pro-moral people, who felt disenfranchised, saw a rallying point, an organization that would speak to the issues they were concerned with but could never get discussed through the liberal-controlled media.[27]

At another point, he claimed that none of his positions were radical thirty years before and noted that he was only seeking "a return to normalcy."[28] Even some liberal critics recognized the importance of this moral force. Dr. Reidar Bjornard of the Northern Baptist Theological Seminary admitted that "the Moral Majority is speaking to issues we should have addressed."[29]

By becoming the Liberty Federation, the Moral Majority lost much of its uniqueness and stumbled into a morass of controversial economic issues that raised little enthusiasm and much division. This uniqueness was both a source of identification and of argument strategy. In viewing the founding of the Liberty Federation, the liberal publication *The Christian Century* noted that, "the Fundamentalist Christians who supported the Moral Majority with regular contributions did so because the group had identified a very specific field that had not previously been cultivated."[30] In the magazine's view, this allowed Falwell to use a highly enthymematic form of argument: "He did not have to argue his case; he merely had to express it in terms that touched deep anxieties."[13] By broadening his appeal to cover the negative effects of the Gramm-Rudman-Hollings budget legislation or the need for a balanced budget amendment to the Constitution, Falwell risked losing much of the organization's uniqueness and its gut-level appeal.

The Reverend Falwell indirectly answered these concerns in two ways. First, he noted that the Moral Majority would continue to function in the same way it always had, as a guardian of moral values. His announcement at the Press Club included the claim that "Moral Majority will be a subsidiary and will continue functioning in the 'strictly moral' areas where we labored in earlier years."[32] Similarly, his first letter to the members guaranteed that "the Moral Majority organization will continue . . . and will maintain its name and its aggressive work in those areas where traditional values are in danger."[33]

Falwell also, less directly, addressed the issue of membership loss by claiming that the Moral Majority's name had been so soiled by the liberal press that people who might otherwise join were deterred from doing so. He argued that:

the press for six years has bloodied and beaten the name, Moral Majority. There are a lot of people who will say yes to everything we are saying, but they dare not stand with us on particular policies for fear of getting tarred, hurt—that is, picking up the baggage the media has dumped on us. But we want to bring these people into our camp.[34]

Implicitly, the decision to abandon the sullied "Moral Majority" name would free these people to associate with the new, untarnished Liberty Federation.

This view is naive. At one level, it seems unlikely that Falwell's liberal opponents would long allow the organization to remain unscathed, especially with Falwell's boast that he would "become more abrasive than ever."[35] Secondly, Falwell failed to recognize the fact that much of the opposition to the organization was directed at Falwell, himself. One popularity survey placed Falwell below Jane Fonda and eighteen other public figures. Democratic strategists have identified their intention to link Republic candidates to Falwell's name, since such linkage has historically produced a flight of voters from the candidate. A poll commissioned by the Free Congress Research and Education Foundation, an arm of a conservative political action committee, surveyed 1,000 people who had voted for Ronald Reagan; they found the 44 percent of voters were "less likely" to vote for an individual whom Falwell had endorsed, with 29 percent "more likely." A survey of registered voters in Virginia showed a more marked effect: only 8 percent were "more likely" to vote for an individual endorsed by Falwell, as opposed to 51 percent who were "less likely" to do so. This same question had been posed in Virginia several times in the past, and an analysis of poll trends showed Falwell's unpopularity had steadily risen to the point where twice as many individuals were "less likely" in 1985 than in 1981. Hence, it is highly questionable whether this name change represented the "strong public relations victory" that the *Christian Century* foresaw.[36]

THE MORAL MAJORITY: SUCCESS OR FAILURE?

We should, in particular, avoid the fallacy of judging the success of the Moral Majority's rhetoric by the ignominious state to which it had fallen. The fact that the Moral Majority ended up in a lowly state may, as Falwell pointed out, indicate its success as easily as its failure. That is, contributions to the organization and active support for its dissipated once its supporters perceived the battle had been won. While this is not necessarily a complete explanation of the organization's decline (the ill-advised decision to rally around support for South Africa and President Marcos of the Philippines may have been as much to blame), it is one that seems consistent with the general decline in contributions to the New Right and neo-conservative organizations.

It may, nonetheless, be possible to argue that the Moral Majority enjoyed some success, even in defeat. This observation is grounded in the organization's original purpose, which was not to be popular but to be successful in reintroducing moral concerns in the political arena. The Moral Majority helped accomplish this. While we cannot parse out the particular effects of this one organization, the conservative movement as a whole has had appreciable success, and the Moral Majority has had a role in it.

We might measure the success of the Moral Majority, not by looking at the success or failure of its specific legislative agenda, but by looking at changes in the very grounds of public debate. This perspective says that the failure of particular Moral Majority initiatives was far less important than the success that the defense of these initiatives had at changing the terms of public debate. We must remember that the function of the Moral Majority was not to lobby for the best compromise it could get, but rather to "take the point" and advance an uncompromising conservative standard. By becoming the most visible and irritating of the representatives of the New Right, the Moral Majority drew considerable fire and enmity to itself and its positions. However, it is possible that by serving as a lightning rod, the organization may have been protecting more modest conservative gains made by more pragmatic groups.

By defending the controversial Family Protection Act, for example, the Moral Majority may have made possible passage of the Hatch Amendments, which controlled the availability of federal funds to education. This occurred in at least two ways. First, the bitter debates over the Family Protection Act helped to draw out and exhaust its liberal opponents. Groups such as the American Civil Liberties Union and the National Education Association had to expend limited political capital to defeat the Family Protection Act, which limited their ability to mount a similar assault on the Hatch Amerndments.[37] Second, the debate served to redefine the terms of political discussion. This meant that long debates over such legislation had the effect of legitimizing further debate on the same question, so that eventually the question shifted from "Does religious morality have a role in public affairs?" to "What role should religious morality play in public affairs?" The shift was subtle but important, because the second question recognized the legitimacy of the conservatives' premises and only went on to ask how those premises might best be implemented.

In the context of our discussion of the Family Protection Act, the question may have shifted from "How should the federal government influence local education choices?" to "Should the federal government influence local education choices?" After hearing about the Family Protection Act for months, the Hatch Amendments (which, technically, just limited the availability of federal funds for psychological testing—which conservatives construed to include everything from values clarification courses to sex education) must have seemed remarkably restrained and sensible. Thus, a critic might claim that the Moral Majority lost because its particular law was not enacted, but would miss the larger point that another bit of the liberal state had been chipped away and another conservative vision ensconced.

Arguably, the Moral Majority and its fellow travelers have effected these changes in a number of public issues. Most visibly, abortion is no longer defended by feminists as a positive good or a liberating experience; it is, at best, a necessary evil. We no longer ask, "Should the schools go back to the basics," but, rather, "What is basic?" Finally, there is no longer any credible political defense of the vision of the Great Society; the prospect of national health insurance has ended, and liberals now debate the degree to which Medicare might be cut. In each of these areas, we now seem to be debating from fundamentally different premises than when first the Moral Majority emerged.

QUESTIONS FOR THE FUTURE

In many ways, the most valuable product of our learning is a better inventory of what we do not know. In examining the rhetoric of the Moral Majority, we have been able to observe rippling change within a broad, continuous flow; our observations permit us to make a few strong conclusions. We might, for example, conclude that much of the effectiveness of the Moral Majority flowed not from its own invention, but from its simple ability to articulate the pent-up frustrations of a great number of ordinary citizens. We might conclude, moreover, that the Moral Majority stayed true to its original vision by deviating little from the core of issues that the Reverend Falwell first articulated in 1979. We might, finally, conclude that the notion of pluralism worked; that is, that the interplay of competing interests served to maintain a long-term stability. Within this framework, the Moral Majority may have served as an essential safety valve, allowing expression of and response to concerns before those concerns posed a credible risk of becoming fundamentally alienating or divisive. The process of pluralism, the political dialectic, does not always operate without rancor, but the fact of its operation serves in the long term to decrease hostility and to legitimize the system. We saw this operating in the Moral Majority, which grew from a coterie of shrill, parochial fundamentalists to an increasingly sophisticated coalition that allowed for the legitimacy of dissent and compromise. These changes were manifested not by surrendering key positions but by learning how one could best defend ardently held beliefs without denying others their beliefs.

There are many questions raised, though. First, how resilient would the political system be against a popular movement espousing radical notions? The Reverend Falwell, for all his bluster, was not a very threatening figure. While his reading of American history was often incorrect, his policies would have done little more than resurrect a period of American history from thirty years ago. Nonetheless, his policies were viewed with the same delicious horror as Swift's *Modest Proposal* and provoked responses about as temperate. The frequent comparisons with Hitler or Khomeini revealed an unpleasant irrationality on the part of liberal and moderate officeholders. Their unwillingness either to treat with Falwell or to acknowledge his maturation confirmed a distressing uninterest in making sure that our political responses were even vaguely realistic. Falwell's most radical tool was voter registration, and his most incendiary authority was the Bible. If such a man can evoke unreasoning panic, then the system's ability to tolerate or respond to a new Populist or Progressive Movement is seriously in doubt.

What are the prospects for a movement espousing fundamental change in society? Falwell started from the religious premise that any number of his opponents paid homage to the Prince of Darkness and ended up dining at the Kennedy reservation on Martha's Vineyard. This may suggest that the pressures for conformity in the system can overwhelm the individual responses to people within it. However much the young Turks in the new religious right ridicule the desire to attend all the right cocktail parties and to be invited onto the *Donahue Show*, many of their leaders appear to have been seduced. In Falwell's case, the man not only dined with the Kennedys and bantered with Donahue, but also helped to judge *People* magazine's 1986 "worst dressed celebrity" contest. Falwell was joined in this undertaking by, among others, a transvestite actor, a rock musician who was highly critical of the Moral Majority and a former bordello operator.[38] In much the same way that regulatory agencies come to be co-opted by the industries they were established to regulate (that is, through daily intercourse and shared travail), it may be that counterelite leaders such as Falwell will be ineluctably drawn to the centers of power and acceptability. We might wonder whether Falwell might have been far more easily tamed if the Establishment had more quickly accepted the validity of his criticisms or the validity of his desire to criticize. By denying him his isolated grandeur, his concerns may have been better channeled and his cultish popularity undercut.

Finally, to what extent is the political system capable of separating the substance of one's claims from the tenor of one's rhetoric? Falwell's positions were not very extreme. The more lunatic suggestions, such as those concerning pornographic pastry and burned books, did not come from the national office or were not long defended in the face of criticism. Falwell's two most controversial policies, opposition to abortion and support for church schools free of government control, were essentially the positions of the Catholic Church. While people chose merely to disagree with Catholic officials supporting these views, they called Falwell "fascist" for defending them. The difference appeared to be that Falwell had not yet learned the proper etiquette of public dispute. As a result, Falwell encountered censure and ridicule where a more savvy operator might have found none.

The Moral Majority was not the first movement to react in visceral disgust at the changes wrought by encroaching social and moral variations. It will not be the last. If its biography teaches us anything, it is that we are at risk of plumbing the depths of irrationality when we confront changes in our dreams. Its warning is that we risk losing control of those dreams unless we reassert the primacy of rationality in our public discourse.

NOTES

1. Jerry Falwell, mass-mailed letter, 6 January 1986.

2. Mary Hanna, "We Haven't Seen the Last of Jerry Falwell," *The Christian Science Monitor*, 22 June 1989, p. 18.

3. Falwell's hometown newspaper, *The News and Daily Advance*, after years of trying, succeeded in getting access to Falwell's financial and tax records. Its investigation showed that Falwell transferred nearly $7 million of Moral Majority receipts to "Old-Time Gospel Hour" accounts between 1984 and 1986, and that the organization's budget fell year by year. The absence of federally required lobbying reports for most of 1984, 1985, and 1986 indicated a lack of political activity. "Religious Ministries Got Chunk of Political Money," *The News and Daily Advance*, 23 August 1987; "Falwell Says Donors Knew Funds Transferred," *The News and Daily Advance*, 25 August 1987.

4. Jeffrey K. Hadden, quoted in "Jerry Falwell Starts a New Political Organization," *Christianity Today*, 7 February 1986, p. 60.

5. Jerry Falwell, mass-mailed letter, 6 January 1986.

6. One measure of the situation was the declining readership of the *Liberty Report*. In the spring and summer of 1985, *Moral Majority Report* claimed a circulation in excess of 1 million issues per month. The claimed circulation for the first issue of *Liberty Report*, contrarily, was just a quarter-million. "Falwell Starts a New Political Organization," p. 60. By its end in 1989, the organization raised only one-quarter as much as the Moral Majority raised in 1984. "Falwell Bids Adieu to Moral Majority," *The Washington Times*, 29 August 1989, p. B1.

7. Falwell's final news conference gave some hint of the sham the organization had become. In addition to Falwell's admission that the group had not been active for years, the simple fact that Falwell announced its demise while President Jerry Nims was not even in the picture suggests the decrepitude of the group. "Moral Majority Disbands with 'Mission Accomplished,' " *Fundamentalist Journal,* July/August 1989, p. 57. *The Liberty Reports,* reduced by then to an eight-page newsletter, abruptly halted publication in June without warning or explanation.

8. "Nationline," *USA Today,* 1 September 1989; "Mark Russell's Washington," *Atlanta Journal,* June 16, 1989.

9. Michael Novak, quoted in "Falwell Aims for a Larger Majority," *Insight,* 20 January 1986, p. 23.

10. Jerry Falwell, *Listen, America!* (New York: Doubleday, 1980).

11. "Falwell Aims for a Larger Majority," p. 22.

12. "Falwell Starts a New Political Organization," p. 60.

13. Jerry Falwell, "Statement to the National Press Club," 3 January 1986, n.p.

14. "Statement to the National Press Club."

15. "Dr. Falwell Forms 'the Liberty Federation,' " *Liberty Report,* January 1986, p. 3.

16. "Falwell Forming Group to Look at Broad Issues," *New York Times,* 4 January 1986, p. 6; interview with Ted Derrick, administrative editor, *Moral Majority Reports,* Lynchburg, VA, 24 May 1985.

17. Ronald Brownstein, "On Paper, Conservative PACs were Tigers in 1984—But Look Again," *National Journal,* 29 June 1985, pp. 1504-1509; "The Decline of Direct Mail," *Washington Post,* 25 May 1985, p. 7.

18. "Falwell Aims for a Larger Majority," p. 22; George Marsden, "Playing Dirty for the Lord?" *The Reformed Journal,* October 1985, p. 7.

19. Jerry Falwell, mass-mailed letter, 13 December 1985.

20. Jerry Falwell, mass-mailed letter, 24 December 1985.

21. "Evangelist Trims Operation," *Rock Island Argus,* 31 March 1986, p. 7.

22. "Falwell Starts a New Political Organization," p. 60.

23. Ibid.

24. "Where Is Jerry Falwell Headed in 1986?" *Christianity Today,* 21 February 1986, p. 39.

25. Derrick interview.

26. "Falwell Aims for a Larger Majority," p. 23.

27. Jerry Falwell, quoted in *Congressional Record,* 25 February 1981, p. E704.

28. Marian Christy, "Reverend Jerry Falwell: Fire and Ice," *Boston Sunday Globe Magazine,* 1 November 1981, p. A29.

29. "Politics of the Moral Majority," *New York Times*, 12 October 1981, p. A17.

30. "a Vision of the Future, Not a Tired Agenda," *The Christian Century*, 22 January 1986, p. 59.

31. "A Vision of the Future," p. 59.

32. "Statement to the National Press Club."

33. Mass-mailed letter, 6 January 1986.

34. "Dr. Falwell Forms 'The Liberty Federation,'" p. 3.

35. Ibid.

36. Edward Walsh, "Democrats Are Saying Some Nasty Things About Falwell—Now They're Calling Him an Ally," *Washington Post National Weekly Edition*, 24 February 1986, p. 15; "Falwell Aims for a Larger Majority," p. 22; "Virginia Polls and Politicians indicate Falwell is Slipping in His Home State," *New York Times*, 24 November 1985, p. 13.

37. Hanna, "We Haven't Seen," p. 18.

38. "Publisher's Letter," *People Weekly*, 1 December 1986, p. 5.

Bibliography

SOURCE MATERIAL FROM THE MORAL MAJORITY

Books and Pamphlets

Falwell, Jerry. Foreword. *The Fundamentalist Phenomenon: The Resurgence of Conservative Christianity.* Ed Dobson, Ed. Grand Rapids, MI: Baker Books, 1982.

_____. *If I Should Die Before I Wake.* Nashville: Thomas Nelson, 1986.

_____. *Listen, America!* New York: Doubleday, 1980.

_____. "Ministers and Marches, 21 March 1965." *God's Bullies.* By Perry Young. New York: Harper, Row & Winston, 1982. 310-317.

_____. *Strength for the Journey.* New York: Pocket Books, 1987.

_____. *What Is the Moral Majority?* Lynchburg, VA, 1980.

Published Interviews

"Where Is Jerry Falwell Headed in 1986?" *Christianity Today* 21 February 1986: 39-41.

"Jerry Falwell, 19 April 1981." *Face the Nation.* Sanford, NC: Microfilming Corporation of America, 1982.

"Interview with the Reverend Jerry Falwell." *Penthouse* March 1981; 58+.

"The Nutshell Interview: Jerry Falwell." *Nutshell. 1981/1982: 34+.*

"An Interview with the Lone Ranger of American Fundamentalism." *Christianity Today* 4 September 1981: 22-27.

Moral Majority Reports

The *Moral Majority Reports* were issued every four weeks or so between March 1980 and June 1982. The July issue was not published, and monthly publication occurred from August 1982 to December 1985. The Moral Majority typically skipped publication in one or two months each year, for no stated reason. The early *Reports* included volume and issue numbers, with the first *Report* being Volume One, Issue Three. In 1984, the *Report* jumped one volume due to a print-setting error. The practice of noting issue and volume was discontinued thereafter.

14 March 1980; 15 August 1980; 11 April 1980; 16 March 1981; 19 January 1981; 16 February 1981; 14 July 1980; November 1983; 30 June 1980; 30 July 1980; 15 October 1980; 17 November 1980; 15 December 1980; 6 June 1980; 26 May 1980; 1 May 1980; 18 May 1981; 22 June 1981; 20 July 1981; 24 August 1981; 21 September 1981; 19 October 1981; 23 November 1981; September 1982; 22 February 1982; 28 June 1982; August 1983; January 1984; February 1984; March 1984; April 1984; May 1984; June 1984; July 1984; August 1984; September 1984; October 1984; November 1984; August 1982; 26 April 1982; November 1982; 24 May 1982; 20 April 1981; October 1982; 28 June 1982; 25 January 1982; 24 May 1982; August 1982; July 1983; September 1983; June 1983; April 1983; May 1983; October 1983; December 1983; September 1983; March 1983; April 1985; January 1985; February 1985; March 1985; July 1985; May 1985; June 1985; August 1985; September 1985; November 1985; 15 September 1980; January 1983.

Liberty Reports

The *Liberty Reports* began appearing monthly from January, 1986. January 1986; February 1986; March 1986; June 1986; July 1986; August 1986; November 1986.

Moral Majority Letters

The fund-raising letters were mailed, on average, once every three weeks. The following collection is incomplete because the Moral Majority will not allow access to its early letters even for its own archives. In addition, some additional mailings were made to the organization's most generous donors. Dates in brackets indicate the approximate time of arrival for undated letters.

22 August 1979; 12 October 1979; 2 July 1980; [June 1981]; 9 February 1981; 15 September 1982; [September 1982]; 1 February 1982; 3 Decem-

ber 1982; 1 March 1982; 12 March 1982; 2 April 1982; 15 April 1982; 14 May 1982; 20 June 1982; 1 July 1982; [July 1982]; 5 August 1982; [August 1982]; 7 September 1982; 1 November 1982; 15 December 1982; 15 February 1982; 23 August 1982; 17 November 1982; 14 October 1983; 12 May 1983; 8 September 1983; 16 December 1983; [January 1983]; [February 1983]; 19 August 1983; August 1983; [January 1983]; 14 January 1983; 8 March 1983; 28 April 1983; 26 May 1983; 15 June 1983; 28 June 1983; 14 July 1983; 30 August 1983; 19 September 1983; 1 November 1983; 16 October 1984; 29 October 1984; 12 November 1984; 12 December 1984; [January 1985]; 20 December 1984; 12 September 1984; 22 August 1984; 9 August 1984; 26 July 1984; 23 May 1984; 15 February 1984; 28 September 1984; 20 June 1984; 15 June 1984; [January 1984]; 9 February 1984; 24 February 1984; 30 April 1984; 28 November 1984; 12 July 1985; 11 January 1985; 1 February 1985; 6 March 1985; 12 February 1985; 13 March 1985; 6 June 1985; 31 May 1985; 1 April 1985; 16 May 1985; 3 May 1985; 25 January 1985; 7 January 1985; 6 January 1986; 15 October 1985; 13 December 1985; 24 December 1985; 2 September 1985; 30 January 1984; 26 May 1983; 4 March 1985; 28 June 1985; 15 November 1983; 28 October 1985; 12 August 1985; 7 November 1985; 26 September 1985; 16 September 1985; 26 August 1985.

Liberty Federation Letters

January 1986; February 1986; 27 February 1986; 14 March 1986; April 1986 (2); May 1986.

Moral Majority Archives

The Moral Majority archives are housed in the Library of Liberty University. The archives mainly hold daily newspapers from the "Old-Time Gospel Hour's clipping service. The archivist estimated that he received 20-50 articles per week, and the articles are stored, unfiled, in stacks of flat boxes. The archive also contained a complete set of the *Moral Majority Reports*, an incomplete set of mass-mailed letters, and the transcripts of the daily *Moral Majority Radio Reports* from 2 January 1984-30 April 1985.

Unpublished Transcripts

Buckelew, Roy. Telephone interview. 6 September 1986.
Derrick, Ted. Personal interview. 25 May 1985.
Falwell, Jerry. Statement to the National Press Club. 3 January 1986.

_____. Transcript of the Columbus, SC, "I Love America" rally. 31 March 1980.

File, Russell. Personal interview. 25 May 1985.

NONMORAL MAJORITY SOURCES

Books

Ackermann, Robert J. *Religion as Critique*. Amherst: The University of Massachusetts Press, 1985.

Adair, John. *Founding Fathers: The Puritans in England and America*. London: J. M. Dent, 1982.

Anderson, Robert M. *Vision of the Disinherited: The Making of American Pentacostalism*. New York: Oxford University Press, 1979.

Bailey, Kenneth K. *Southern White Protestantism in the Twentieth Century*. New York: Harper & Row, 1964.

Bercovitch, Sacvan. *The American Jeremiad*. Madison: University of Wisconsin Press, 1978.

Blanke, Gustav. "Puritan Contributions to the Rhetoric of America's Mission." *Studies in New England Puritanism*. W. Herget, Ed. New York: Peter Lang, 1983.

Bromley, David G. and Anson D. Shupe, Eds. *New Christian Politics*. Macon, GA: Mercer University Press, 1984.

Conway, Flo and Jim Siegelman. *Holy Terror*. New York: Dell, 1984.

Cox, Harvey G. *Religion in the Secular City*. New York: Simon and Schuster, 1984.

Crawford, Alan. *Thunder on the Right*. New York: Random House, 1980.

D'Souza, Dinesh. *Falwell Before the Millennium: A Critical Biography*. Lake Bluff, IL: Regnery-Gateway, 1984.

Douglas, Mary T. and Steven M. Tipton, Eds. *Religion and America*. Boston: Beacon Press, 1983.

Finch, Phillip. *God, Guts and Guns*. New York: Seaview Press, 1983.

Fitzgerald Frances. *Cities on a Hill*. New York: Simon & Schuster, 1986.

Goodman, William R. and James J. H. Price. *Jerry Falwell: An Authorized Profile*. Lynchburg, VA: Paris and Associates, 1981.

Guth, James L. "The Politics of the Christian Right." *Interest Group Politics*. Allan Cigler and Burdett Loomis, Eds. Washington: Congressional Quarterly Press, 1983.

Hadden, Jeffrey and Charles Swann. *Prime-Time Preachers*. Reading, MA: Addison-Wesley, 1981.

Hammond, John L. *The Politics of Benevolence: Revival Religion and American Voting Behavior*. Norwood, NJ: Ablex Publishing, 1979.

Harrell, David E. *All Things Are Possible: The Healing and Charismatic Revivals in Modern America.* Bloomington: Indiana University Press, 1975.

Hill, Samuel and Dennis Owen. *The New Religious-Political Right in America.* Nashville: Abingdon Press, 1982.

Hofstadter, Richard. *Anti-intellectualism in American Life.* New York: Vintage Books, 1963.

Jorstad, Erling. *The Politics of Moralism.* Minneapolis: Augsburg, 1981.

Leuchtenberg, William E. "The New Deal and the Analogue of War," *Change and Continuity in Twentieth-Century America.* John Braeman, Robert Bremner, and Everett Walters, Eds. Columbus: Ohio State University Press, 1964. 81-143.

Liebman, Robert C. and Robert Wuthnow, Eds. *The New Christian Right.* Hawthorne, NY: Aldine Publishing, 1983.

McIntyre, Thomas J. *The Fear Brokers.* Boston: Beacon Press, 1979.

McLoughlin, William G. *Billy Sunday Was His Real Name.* Chicago: University of Chicago Press, 1955.

_____. *Revivals, Awakenings and Reform.* Chicago: University of Chicago Press, 1978.

Maguire, Daniel. *The New Subversives.* New York: Continuum, 1982.

Marsden, George. *Fundamentalism and American Culture: The Shaping of Twentieth-Century Evangelicalism, 1870-1925.* New York: Oxford University Press, 1980.

Phillips, Kevin P. *Post-conservative America.* New York: Random House, 1982.

Pines, Burton. *Back to Basics.* Washington, D.C.: The Heritage Foundation, 1982.

Pingry, Patricia. *Jerry Falwell: Man of Vision.* Milwaukee: Ideals Publishing, 1980.

Rosten, Leo, Ed. *Religions of America.* New York: Simon and Schuster, 1975.

Saloma, John S. *Ominous Politics.* New York: Hill and Wang, 1984.

Schaeffer, Francis A. *A Christian Manifesto.* Westchester, IL: Crossway Books, 1981.

Shupe, Anson and William Stacey. *Born-Again Politics.* New York: Edward Mellen Press, 1982.

Stein, Ben. *The View from Sunset Boulevard.* New York: Basic Books, 1979.

Strober, Jerry and Ruth McClellan. *The Jerry Falwell Story.* New York: Ibex Publishing, 1982.

Tuchman, Barbara. *The Proud Tower: A Portrait of the World Before the War.* New York: Macmillan, 1966.

Tuveson, Ernest L. *Redeemer Nation: The Idea of America's Millennial Role.* Chicago: University of Chicago Press, 1968.

Viguerie, Richard A. *The New Right: We're Ready to Lead.* Falls Church, VA: The Viguerie Company, 1980.

Webber, Robert. *The Moral Majority: Right or Wrong?* Westchester, IL: Good News Publishing, 1981.

Willoughby, William. *Does America Need the Moral Majority?* South Plainfield, NJ: Bridge Publishing, 1981.

Young, Perry D. *God's Bullies.* New York: Harper, Row & Winston, 1982.

Zwier, Robert. *Born-Again Politics.* Downers Grove, IL: Inter-varsity Press, 1982.

Doctoral Dissertations

Brenner, Douglas F. "The Rhetoric of the Moral Majority: Transforming Perceptions of Opposition." Diss. University of Nebraska-Lincoln, 1984.

Buckelew, Roy E. "The Political Preaching of Jerry Falwell: A Rhetorical Analysis of the Political Preaching of Rev. Jerry Falwell in Behalf of the Moral Majority During the 1980 Political Campaign." Diss. University of Southern California, 1983.

Jefferson, Patricia A. "Spokesmen for a Holy Cause: A Rhetorical Examination of Selected Leaders of the New Religious-Political Right." Diss. Indiana University, 1984.

Phipps, Kim S. "The Rhetoric of the Moral Majority Movement: A Case Study and Reassessment of Conservative Resistance." Diss. Kent State University, 1985.

Ray, Vernon O. "Rhetorical Analysis of the Political Preaching of the Reverend Jerry Falwell: The Moral Majority Sermons, 1979." Diss. The Louisiana State University, 1985.

Journal Articles

Clouse, Robert G. "The New Christian Right, America, and the Kingdom of God." *Christian Scholar's Review* 11 (1982): 3-16.

Conley, Carolyn. " 'Make Full Proof of Thy Ministry': Lamarr Mooneyham, the Tri-City Baptist Temple, and the Moral Majority." *South Atlantic Quarterly* 81 (1982): 131-146.

Conrad, Charles. "The Rhetoric of the Moral Majority: An Analysis of Romantic Form." *Quarterly Journal of Speech* 69 (1983): 159-170.

Day-Lower, Donna. "Who Is the Moral Majority? A Composite Profile." *Union Seminary Quarterly Review* 37 (1983): 335-349.

Dayton, Donald W. "Some Perspectives on 'The New Christian Right.' " *Fides et Historia* 15 (1982): 54-60.

Hadden, Jeffrey K. and Charles E. Swann. "Responding to the Christian Right." *Theology Today* 39 (1983): 377-384.

Hall, Cline E. and Jerry Combee. "The Moral Majority: Is It a New Ecumenicalism?" *Foundations* 25 (1982): 204-211.

Harrell, David E. "The Roots of the Moral Majority: Fundamentalism Revisited." Occasional Papers, The Institute for Ecumenical and Cultural Research 15 (1981): 1-12.

Johnson, Stephen D. and Joseph B. Tamney. "The Christian Right and the 1980 Presidential Election." *Journal for the Scientific Study of Religion* 21 (1982): 123-131.

_____. "Support for the Moral Majority: A Test of a Model." *Journal for the Scientific Study of Religion* 23 (1984): 183-196.

Johnston, Edwin D. "Social Scientists Examine the New Religious Right." *Teaching Political Science* 12 (1984): 4-11.

Jorstad, Erling. "The New Christian Right." *Theology Today* 38 (1981): 193-200.

Lienesch, Michael. "The Paradoxical Politics of the Religious Right." *Soundings* 66 (1983): 70-99.

_____. "Right-Wing Religion: Christian Conservatism as a Political Movement." *Political Science Quarterly* 97 (1982): 403-425.

_____. "The Role of Political Millennialism in Early American Nationalism." *Western Political Quarterly* 36 (1983): 445-465.

McLoughlin, Wiliam G. "Faith." *American Quarterly* 35 (1983): 101-115.

_____. "The Illusions and Dangers of the New Christian Right." *Foundations* 25 (1982): 128-143.

Mueller, Carol. "In Search of a Constituency for the 'New Religious Right.' " *Public Opinion Quarterly* 47 (1983): 213-229.

Roberts, Churchill L. "Attitudes and Media Use of the Moral Majority." *Journal of Broadcasting* 27 (1983): 403-410.

Ruegsegger, Ron. "Francis Schaeffer on Philosophy." *Christian Scholar's Review* 10 (1981): 238-259.

Simons, Herbert. "Requirements, Problems and Strategies: A Theory of Persuasion for Social Movements." *Quarterly Journal of Speech* 56 (1970): 1-11.

Tamney, Joseph P. and Stephen D. Johnson. "The Moral Majority in Middletown." *Journal for the Scientific Study of Religion* 22 (1983): 145-157.

Tucker, Bruce. "The Reinterpretation of Puritan History in Provincial New England." *The New England Quarterly* 54 (1981): 481-498.

Whitfield, Stephen J. " 'One Nation Under God': The Rise of the Religious Right." *Virginia Quarterly Review* 58 (1982): 557-574.

Wood, James E. "Religious Fundamentalism and the New Right." *Journal of Church and State* 22 (1980): 409-421.

Yinger, J. Milton and Stephen Cutler. "The Moral Majority Viewed Sociologically." *Sociological Focus* 15 (1982): 289-305.
Zimmerman, A. L. "Thunder Everywhere: The Developing Rhetoric of Jerry Falwell." *Speaker and Gavel* 19 (1981-1982): 22-28.

Magazine Articles

"As Moral Majority Girds for '82 Elections." *U.S. News and World Report* 21 June 1982: 43-44.
Bennett, John C. "Assessing the Concerns of the Religious Right." *The Christian Century* 14 October 1981: 1018-1022.
"Born-Again Politics: The Dallas Briefing." *Presbyterian Life* 20 October 1980: 5-6.
Brown, Robert M. "Listen, Jerry Falwell!" *Christianity & Crisis* 22 December 1980: 360-364.
Brownstein, Ronald. "On Paper, Conservative PACs Were Tigers in 1984—But Look Again." *National Journal* 29 June 1985: 1504-1509.
Carlin, David R. "Politics and Religion." *America* 27 October 1984: 248.
Castelli, Jim. "Has the Christian Right Peaked?" *Church and State* October 1981: 17-18.

Newspapers and Newspaper Files

National Newspaper Index, January 1976-October 1986, inclusive. This service indexes the nation's major newspapers, including *The New York Times, Washington Post, Christian Science Monitor, Wall Street Journal,* and *Los Angeles Times.*

Television Indexes

CBS News Index. New York: Microfilming Corporation of America, 1981.
Television News Index and Abstracts. Nashville: Vanderbilt University, 1979-1985.

Unpublished Papers

Alexander, Alison, W. Barnett Pearce, Brian Duke, Sheryl Perlmutter Bowen, and Kyung-what Kang. "The Social Construction of the Moral Majority, Part 2: Changed Practices and Continuous Structure in Social Interaction." ICA Convention. Dallas, May 1983.
Bowen, Sheryl Perlmutter, W. Barnett Pearce, and Alison Alexander. "The Social Construction of the Moral Majority, Part 1: Some

Characteristics of the Moral Majority's Social Reality.'' ECA Convention. Ocean City, April 1983.

Brummett, Barry. "The Dramatic Substance of Metaphor in Politics.'' SCA Convention. Louisville, November 1982.

_____. "The Rhetoric of the Apocalyptic.'' SCA Convention. Washington, November 1983.

Burnett, Nicholas F. S. "Like Having a Water Moccasin for a Watchdog: Ethical Grounds and Devious Means in the Rhetoric of the National Conservative Political Action Committee.'' SCA Convention. Chicago, November 1984.

Copeland, Gary A. "Four Types of Church Attendance and Opinions on Fundamentalist, Black and Government Issues.'' SCA Convention. Washington, November 1983.

Cutbirth, Craig and Mark Schmidt. "Direct Mail as a Rhetorical Tool: The Conservative Campaign of 1980.'' SCA Convention. Anaheim, November 1981.

Duffy, Bernard K. "The Anti-Humanist Rhetoric of the New Religious Right.'' SCA Convention. Washington, November 1983.

Dunn. Marvin G. "The Resurrection of Ideology: Religion, Legitimacy, and the American Enterprise.'' Society for the Scientific Study of Religion Convention. Providence, R.I., October 1982.

Fadely, Dean and Ralph Hamlett. "The Three Faces of Jerry Falwell.'' SCA Convention. Washington, November 1983.

Fairbank, James D. "The Evangelical Right: Beginnings of Another Symbolic Crusade?'' American Political Science Association Convention. New York, September 1981.

Hahn, Dan F. and Naomi Welsner. "The Paranoid Style of the Fundamentalist Far Right.'' SCA Convention. New York, November 1982.

Hoover, Stewart M. "Religious Media, Religious Activity and Conventional Media Use as Leisure Activities.'' SCA Convention. Washington, November 1983.

Simpson, John H. "Is There a Moral Majority?'' Society for the Scientific Study of Religion Convention. Baltimore, November 1981.

Tucker, David E. "Local Religious Broadcasting: Great Waste or Great Opportunity?'' SCA Convention. Washington, November 1983.

Virts, Paul H. and J. D. Keeler. "Audiences and Their Perceptions of Religious Television Broadcasters.'' SCA Convention. Washington, November 1983.

Weisner, Naomi R. and Dan Hahn. "On the Social Consequences of the Fusion of Authoritarian Religion and Pluralistic Politics.'' Provided by the authors with no further identification.

Index

ABOUT THE AUTHOR

DAVID SNOWBALL is a native of Wilkinsburg, Pennsylvania, and was educated in the public schools there. He received his B.A. from the University of Pittsburgh and his M.A. and Ph.D. from the University of Massachusetts. His academic training is in the history and criticism of public address.

Snowball has been a member of the faculty of Augustana College in Rock Island, Illinois, since 1984. He is the Chair of the Department of Speech Communication and of the Division of Fine and Performing Arts, as well as Director of Debate.